ONE DROP OF FOREVER
AMELIA AND HER ANGEL

Donielle Ingersoll

ISBN Paperback   978-1-965126-09-7
ISBN Hardback   978-1-965126-10-3
ISBN eBook   978-1-965126-11-0

Printed in the United States of America.

www.eastwenatcheepublishing.com

CONTENTS

PROLOGUE

Cassandra looked out the window. The Montana evening looked warm and friendly for the middle of January. It probably wasn't though. A full moon was rising off in east over the neighbor's cabin. She took out her camera. It had a 600mm lens that could bring the moon in close. It was beautiful!

The cabin with the moon and trees looked like a Stephen Lyman painting without the warm fire glow from the windows. That would have made the photo picture perfect. No one was home to turn them on, however. There was a polarizer lens that she spun around several times, snapping off half a dozen photos. The camera also had a timer. After getting the initial shots, she set the timer to take a photo every five minutes for the next three hours. This way, she could catch the moon as it rose higher in the sky. The nice thing about the timer was she could go do stuff and the photos would come automatically.

It was time to do the chores. The expectant mother made her way slowly over to the rack and started working the coat back and forth to free it from its hook. The last time she placed it up there, she failed to recognize that the strings that came down from its hood were still tied together. They had caught on the hardware, and although the hood came free, the ties did not want to. She was too short, that was the problem. Her husband who towered above her could have lifted it off in a second, but he was uptown on some last-minute business. An emergency had come up or so, his secretary had said. This was not supposed to happen. You see, Cassandra was overdue, two days overdue in fact. Amelia did not want to leave her cozy home. For over nine months, she had been perfectly content to stay there and absorb the warmth and love of her mother.

Maybe if I take the Polaris up to the goat barn, I can break the ice off their water and make certain they are okay, the young mother thought to herself as she gave one more tug on the jacket. This time, the ties separated, and it partially covered her head as it followed the commands of gravity,

1

tumbling earthward. What goes up must come down, and it did, her thoughts continued as she put first one arm in a sleeve and then the other. The jacket was just too small. What has happened to this? Has it shrunk? It is filled with down though. Does down shrink? Just then Amelia gave a swift kick and set the record straight. Oh, silly me, of course, the coat is too small. It must cover two of us now, the thoughts transformed into a conversation between mother and daughter.

"Amelia, my sweet, sweet little girl. Why are you being so hard on me? Your daddy and I have been looking forward to meeting you face to face for the last nine plus months. We got so excited yesterday when—" a contraction ripped through the little mother, and she had to take a deep breath to fight off the pain. "That was a good one, Amelia. A few more of those and we will see you for sure, or I will go crazy."

The Polaris RMK 800 snowmobile was facing out the garage as the expectant mother came down the steps. Her husband had rigged up an automatic start, so she did not need to pull the cord. After turning the key to the right position, she pushed the button and was rewarded with the purring of the engine. The garage door was opened now, and Cassandra could see that the sky had played a trick on her.

As the engine of the sled warmed, she noticed there were tiny crystals falling from the heavens, and they were cold. A few of them landed on her nose as well as the rest of her face. She instinctively ran her tongue up and licked a few flakes off that landed above her lips. She decided to run the top of her M-mission over her hair and the bottom of it up on her face before climbing on the machine and riding up the hill. It was about an eighth of a mile to the old red barn. The builder had positioned it in a natural gully so the prevailing north to westerly winds would blow over only the upper portion of it as they came off the Bridger Mountain Range. That kept the part of the barn where the animals found shelter more protected from the cold of winter or the heat of summer.

The former owners had cattle that grazed over all 120 acres. Mike and Cassandra had goats. A portion of the property was refenced. There were still some old rotten fence posts in the rest of the area, and you could find some rusty barbed wire there also. These marked the property line. The sled slid easily unto the snow, and she maneuvered the corner with the handles as more of the tiny crystals sparkled down from the

2

heavens. The crystals must have been the cause of the rainbow she saw around the moon when taking the photos.

There was a large mercury lamp that gave light to the entire area. It came on at dusk and showed all night. Not only did it allow them to work in the evening, but it also was a deterrent for wild animals. A bear coming out of winter hibernation was hungry enough to eat a goat if they wanted to. The light helped keep them away. At the pen, she took a crowbar and broke the ice in the barrel. It was not that thick. The goats normally would have been able to break through it without a problem. Their survival instinct would assure them of that.

A nanny came over and started licking the little crystals of ice off her shoulder as she bent to pull her snow pants down over her boots. She noticed the barrel containing some grain was partially chewed through. Mike would need to do something with it soon, or they would be spilling all over the place. Five more goats came over to get some attention as she stood up again. One would also be a mother soon. By the looks of it, she would have twins.

While out there, she really needed to milk two of the other goats. She got the equipment, found the bench, and soon was in position. With a little bit of effort, the task was done, and number 2 was in position. Another contraction rocked her body, causing her to double over. Something was wrong, really wrong! This was not normal. At the same time, she heard the wind pick up in intensity as it started whistling over the roof of the building.

There was one more thing she should do—get the tarp down over the main opening. They could close the door if need be. It was on rollers but very rusty. Her husband could move it, or she could hook the 4x4 up to it and pull it shut, if necessary, but the tarp was easier. Mike kept it rolled up so the goats would not eat it. She set the milk out of reach of the kids and pulled the first rope with no problem at all, but the second one gave her trouble even as her coat had. Finally, it came loose, and the front of the building was covered. The goats would be warm in the straw, even if the temperatures dropped below zero. They had water and feed.

Recovering the milk, she was soon back on the snowmobile. It roared to life, and she started back to the house. Unfortunately, going back was not the easy ride she expected.

Something happened to the throttle. It was so quick the soon-to-be mother found herself in a giant drift before she had time to think. The sled had left her stranded there as it continued flying down the hill. There was no way she was going down there to get that machine. It buried itself in another drift while she struggled to gain her footing. She looked around for the milk. It was just out of reach. Thankfully the lid had not come off. She stretched as far as she could toward it, and being off balanced, she was rewarded with falling face-first into the snow. It was cold. She could just reach the handle and pulled the container toward her.

At last, she was up and started waddling back to the house. Occasionally, her feet would slip out from under her, and she would find herself on her bottom. With every bump like that, Amelia grew more and more uncomfortable in her cozy little den. Another sharp pain rocked the lady as she was on the ground for the third time. Then her water broke. She still had a way to go. Waddling first one way and then the other, she finally reached the door. She realized that the little bit of water that had managed to escape from inside her clothes was frozen. Part of one boot had received a generous portion of it also. Inside, she worked her way out of her bundles and went to the mirror to examine what had happened.

The baby wanted to come out, but something was preventing her. Instinctively, she reached for her cell phone. The neighbor lady had been placed on notice for such a time as this. At first sign of something changing, she would take Cassandra to the hospital. It was close to where Mike had gone so he could be there in a moment's notice. The cell phone was missing. It must have slipped out of her pocket when she reached for the milk. The contractions were coming faster and faster as the little fat-bellied lady made her way to the bathroom and started running some warm water in the tub. With frozen fingers and a half-frozen face, perhaps a bath would help, perhaps not. Somewhere back in a giant snowdrift at that very moment, her iPhone was ringing.

***

Mike looked at his watch. The manager was late for his appointment again. This had to stop. It was the third time this had happened in a week. Every time, Jim came up with some excuse as to why it had happened and apologized profusely. He promised it would not happen again. But it always did. Had he not been good at some other things the business needed, he would not have been needed. But Jim knew the ropes better than anyone else in the firm. Except for being tardy, the rest of his skills were honed to perfection. He could get more done in an hour than any other two people. He decided to call Cassandra and see if anything had developed. The late arrival of their daughter was concerning. What if she was having complications? When her voicemail came on, he stopped the call. She was not able to get around as fast as usual with the baby coming, so he did not call her back right away. She would probably waddle over to the phone and call him in a few minutes.

He went into the office and was surprised to see a window open. A strong wind was blowing the curtains back and forth as ice crystals made unusual patterns on the floor. The screen had been removed, and as he looked toward his desk, there were papers scattered all over the floor. Had someone broken into his office and taken something? There was an upturned wastebasket in the mess also. The remains of yesterday's lunch were mixed in with important files. Catchup was smeared across another set of papers that were supposed to have been sent off in the mail yesterday. Now the secretary would need to reprint them, and that would make them even later as the mail here was always forwarded to the next large city even if it needed to be delivered a few blocks away.

A bit of anger started to swell up in his mind as he passed through the office and entered the break room. There, on the floor face down was Jim. Mike ran over and knelt by him. His flesh was cold. That could mean only one thing, he was dead. This would not go very well with the police. If anyone in the building had even thought there was trouble between the two men, he would be the chief suspect. A letter opener was sticking out from his chest. He had been stabbed. Mike reached for his phone and called 911. The sooner this got reconciled, the sooner he could figure out what to do next, if there would be a next.

***

Some twenty miles away, Cassandra's mother picked up her cell phone and called her daughter. She was supposed to be there at the house when her first grandchild came into the world. They had planned this for months. She had even started toward the place and gotten down the road several miles when the old VW Beetle decided it had a plan of its own. It was even now in the shop getting some new gaskets. A lot of oil had leaked out of the engine over the last several weeks. Had it not been made back in the days when they really made cars tough, it quite possibly would not have survived the crisis. But few cars were made better, and so it was just a matter of time. Since the mechanic did not usually work on Volkswagens, there were parts that needed to be ordered. They had to come in from Billings.

Grandmother was pleased the little girl had decided to hold off on her entrance into the world. It would be so nice to have them all together when she first introduced herself. The phone went to voicemail. Must be she was on another call? Five minutes later, the mechanic called and said the car was ready. He apologized for the delay, and to make up for it was, at that very moment, driving to her house. His assistant was following in his car so they would have a ride back. He assured her he would be there shortly. Milly went over and checked her suitcase one more time. It appeared that everything she needed was there. Then she remembered her boots. She probably better get a heavy coat also as the weather had taken a turn for the worst. Twenty minutes later, she was heading for her daughter's home. If the roads were good, she would be there shortly.

***

When Cassandra did not answer the phone, the neighbor who had been waiting for a call got in her SUV and drove the short distance to Mike's place. As she started up the driveway, however, the car slipped off the road, and she found herself stuck in the snow that had been pushed there by the plough. Exiting the vehicle, she made her way up the slippery road. At the steps, she paused to catch her breath. It was quite a hill. Five steps later, she was ringing the doorbell. When nobody answered, she let herself in. Hearing noise in the bathroom, she made her way there. What she found was shocking. Sitting on the floor with some blood around, she found Cassandra rocking back and forth with pain.

Julie was training to be a midwife. She had a few classes under her belt but was nowhere near qualified to bring a baby into the world if it did not happen naturally. She could tell in a minute this one would not come naturally. She felt the woman's tummy and decided that Amelia was in the wrong position. The wrong part of her body was trying to come first. Julie sterilized her hands and tried to push the little one back. She was a stubborn baby. After some less-than-gentle persuasion, she began to cooperate. The midwife-to-be had taken a class where a lifelike doll had been placed inside a mock womb. They had tried to make it as real as possible, even adding moisture and heat. The students had all taken turns turning the lifelike doll this way and that to position it to come. And so, with only that experience, the process began.

All the time, Julie was talking to Cassandra, comforting her, encouraging her, trying to sooth her nerves as her pain seemed to increase. About the time she had the little girl into position, her phone rang. With one hand inside and another soothing the soon-to-be mother, she could not answer it. She noticed that it was Mike. He needed to know what was happening. He also needed to know that his wife would not be going to the hospital. This little one would come into the world in her own home. She gave one more gentle push, and Amelia was positioned for her passage. Sometimes this could happen quickly, sometimes it might take a while. She removed her hand and decided to let nature take its course if that were possible. If not, she might need to do some surgery to help her out. Washing her hands, she picked up her phone and called. The 911 hotline received another call shortly after the one that had occurred minutes before. Nobody there knew, however, the two calls were even remotely connected.

***

Milly made great time on the road. The traffic was light, and the roads had enough bare pavement to make the trip without the problems that could have been in place had Murphy's Law continued to play out its hand. But perhaps enough was enough? She reached the driveway in record time and went barreling by the stuck SUV, skidding to a stop by the front steps. She was surprisingly agile for an older woman. She took the stairs two at a time and, without knocking, entered the door.

She found her daughter more comfortable now. She was no longer on the bathroom floor but on the bed. A piece of plastic had been placed under the expectant mother with a sheet over it, and Julie was wiping her forehead with a warm washcloth. The more-experienced mother went right to work. She drew some hot water from the faucet and had some clean towels and washcloths out in a jiffy. The contractions were coming more and more rapidly now. The little head was trying to push its way through when the ambulance arrived. Three medics came in, and the two ladies were glad to turn the process over to the pros. If all went well, Amelia would soon be feeding at her mother's breast.

***

When the police arrived at the office, however, things were not going so good for Mike. They were putting him through some tough talk. Whatever happened to 'innocent until proven guilty'? About that time, his phone rang. The police would not let him answer it. When the name Julie came up, they asked him who she was.

"It is my mother-in-law. My wife is probably having our baby right now." That news seemed to soften the men in blue up a little, and they turned it over to him to answer.

"You need to get home as fast as you can, Mike. Cassandra is delivering your daughter right now. She never made it to the hospital. They may need to do some special work on her. It is critical, but the medics are here and have assured us that the mother and baby have a great chance of making it if the process can be completed in ten, no less than twenty minutes. Why aren't you here beside my daughter? No girl should be going through this without the other half of the reason it is happening in the first place!"

Mom was not very happy with him. That was certain. About that time, the coroner arrived, and the policeman who had been the hardest on the man spoke, "Jim is not going

8

anywhere soon, Mike. If your wife is having a baby, you need to be there by her side. I will get you there in no time. The detective will take the apparent murder weapon down to the lab and look around for any more evidence he can find. Let's get that baby born."

A lady policewoman jumped in the car with them, and with lights flashing, they were off.

***

CHAPTER 1
Amelia and the Crow

Amelia and her mother had hiked up to the spring. It flowed year around unless the weather got too cold in the winter, then a spongy sheet of ice would form over it. You needed to be careful in walking on that sheet. If you broke through the ice, you could get not only muddy boots but also could sink in up above your waistline. There was no ice today, however. It was a beautiful spring morning. They had gone looking for wildflowers. The earliest ones like spring beauties and avalanche lilies were already gone. They found a few remaining buttercups, shooting stars, but the bitterroots were just coming into bloom along with the larkspurs. They also found some skunk cabbages.

A moose and her calf came to the spring to drink, but seeing the people there, they quickly retreated up the hill. Following their movement, Amelia spotted a crow making a fuss over something on the forest floor. She and her mother went over to take a closer look. A baby crow too small to leave the nest was on the ground. It did not look very good. It was nearly dead. Its little mouth was open, and it was gasping for breath. The little girl took it over to the water, and with her finger, she got a few drops into its throat. It seemed to help. The little one snuggled down in her hands. Since there was no way to place it back in the nest, Amelia decided to try and take it back home.

"This little bird will die if I do not help it, Mother. We need to take it back to the house, and I will feed it and nurse it back to health."

Her mother shook her head not in opposition to the idea her daughter had but because she knew the chances of it surviving were not very good. "I suppose you can try, Amy, but very few of them will live once in captivity. You do realize you will have to feed it several times a day, don't you? Baby birds keep both of their parents busy most of the time trying to keep them fed. This one has developed a good set of wings, so it is probably about two weeks out from the time it should be leaving the nest."

"I will not let it die. It will live and be my pet bird."

"Do you realize that crows or ravens can be real pest once they are tamed?"

The mother and daughter were heading back to the house as she asked the question. Either the mother or father crow were following them, making a lot of noise. Cassandra was wondering if the bird was old enough to survive away from its nest. Its parents knew where it was. They were far better equipped to care for it than her daughter. Then again, Amelia was a determined child.

Back at the house, the little girl mixed up some bread and goat's milk. The baby crow was placed in a box in a warm spot. It did eat the bread and milk until it had enough then settled down for a nap. Amy sat next to it, watching for any problems. After a little over an hour, it was hungry again, so she fed it. But a little bit later, it opened its mouth again like it was dying. The last time she had seen it do that, some water helped. But the water did not do any good. She had heard of mouth-to-mouth respiration. Did it need air? She placed her mouth over that of the bird and tried to put some air in it. That did not work, so not knowing what else to do, she gave a little sucking motion. A wad of bread and milk came up its throat along with the remains of some type of insect or lizard that was hard and stringy. She spit it out quickly, and the bird settled back down to normal. That was its nearest brush with death.

Because of the little girl's persistence, it grew into a pet. Wherever she went, the bird went. It sat on her shoulder and let her know when it was hungry. It also developed a playful spirit. One of its favorite things to do was bite her ear lobe. It was not a hard bite, but the first time it happened, Amelia was surprised.

After studying things out, she decided it was a male. That required a boy's name. What do you name a boy pet? She did not want it to sound like a cat or a dog but a person. Finally, she settled on the name Rex. Over the next several weeks, they became the best of friends. She would open the window in her bedroom so it could come and go as it pleased. Shortly after Rex learned to fly, he also learned to supply most of his own food. He would gather it from outside, and of course, the scraps from the dinner table were always welcomed. He became very fond of portions of Amelia's bread crusts. He also potty trained himself after taking flight for the first time.

Since her dad was in prison for the murder of his manager, she and her mom had to run the farm by themselves. They had to feed the goats twice a day. Amy learned to milk them also after she was old enough. There was income coming in from her dad's business. Uncle Henry had stepped in to fill in the gap. He was a jolly uncle and tried his best to fill the shoes of a father for the little girl, but he had to split his time between her and his own two children. Cassandra filled the position of the former secretary. Henry did not like the former employee. Neither did he trust her. She had acted strange after the murder. Three sets of fingerprints were taken off the letter opener. There were Joyce's, Mike's, and Jim's. Joyce had an alibi. She claimed to be at home baking pies when the murder occurred. Her lawyer brought in three of the recipients who had received the pies to testify that the secretary had indeed made them. Mike did not have an alibi. He was at the scene of the crime. They said he opened the window, scattered the papers around, and spilled food over them to make it appear like someone had gained access to the building by that means. An autopsy showed signs of a mild sedative in Jim's body. A nearby cup of coffee also contained it. So the manager had been sedated to a point where he could not struggle much, and then he was stabbed while still under the influence of the drugs.

After firing Joyce, Henry had found evidence that she and the manager had been doing some shady deals between themselves. They had embezzled money from an account that was not even on the records. He also found that a possible affair was going on between them, even though Joyce was married. It made sense. The two of them had traveled to different states. There were conventions to go to and trade shows. Though he could not prove it, Henry expected they often had shared the same hotel room on these trips. Jim had never married, and Joyce, for all practical purposes, was an attractive woman. She had a way of flirting when she wanted something, even with Mike at times. She would put on her charms and be a pristine secretary for a few days, getting everything done ahead of time and in perfect order. Then she would try and manipulate her boss to do as she wished in one or two areas, pointing out how it would benefit not only the business but him personally. After a few times, Mike did not fall for it anymore, but Jim? He was a different matter. She had him wrapped around her pretty little finger. He would march around and do almost anything she asked or find a way to sidetrack her when he knew what she wanted was not going to happen.

Cassandra also made money with her photographs. She was quite the photographer. Many days were spent in Yellowstone National Park searching for animals she could photograph. She also captured waterfall pictures from various areas and made calendars of them. She received a contract with a large company that wanted to showcase her wild animal and bird photos. After Rex came into their lives, she got several photographs of him also and did a raven calendar. She could, of course, get really close to this bird. On one set of calendars, she showcased several log cabins out in the wilds of nature. She liked to photograph the more rustic-looking ones—the ones that looked like some hermit had built them and lived way off in the woods somewhere seemingly untouched by the modern world. She also photographed old barns. The one on their property was as beautiful as it was rugged. It always had first place on her barn calendars.

One day, the little mother became very worried when Rex came back without his companion. He was making all kinds of fuss. He had also learned some words. While the mother and daughter were working on projects together, the bird had picked up the words "Rex help?" He actually would go and bring things to them such as he could carry in his beak and ask if he could help, "Rex help, Rex help." Sometimes it did help them, but most of the time, the things he brought were useless.

Today, he flew and landed on the shoulder of Cassandra and just said, "Help." No matter how hard he tried, he could not pronounce "Amelia," or even the name her mother used more often for her daughter "Amy." When it came out, it sounded like "Ahmil." So when he landed on the mother's shoulder and said, "Help Ahmil," the mother became very concerned. After saying the phrase a couple of times, he flew up in the air and started flying toward the top of the hill. When Cassandra did not follow, he did it again with more urgency in his voice if a bird can speak in an urgent voice, "Help Ahmil, help Ahmil." Finally, she got the hint and started walking up the mountain.

13

Then she thought if something was wrong, how would she get the girl back down? So she went over toward the goat barn and uncovered the ATV. Rex settled down on her shoulder again and spoke, "Help, help Ahmil."

"I am going to help her, Rex. I am going to take the 4x4 up there in case I need a way to get her back to the house." She could not imagine she was trying to explain herself to a bird, but he seemed to understand and settled down. In a little bit, she was following him up to the tree line. Going as far as she could with the vehicle, she then followed him on foot a little way into the forest. There, she saw her daughter lying on the ground, seemingly unresponsive. Running over to her, she checked her pulse. It was weak, but she was alive. Cradling the little one in her arms, she took her back to the ATV and made her way down to the house. Amelia would moan every so often, as if she was in pain. Since the hospital was only fifteen minutes away, the little mother drove her daughter to the ER. They took her in right away. She was thankful there was not an entire room filled with people waiting to get in. As she looked at her little sweetheart all white and quiet, a fear came over Cassandra. This was not like Amy at all. Something was drastically wrong.

Rex did not like it when the family left the ranch. He would make a big fuss and cry out, "Rex go, Rex go!" Sometimes they would take him along with them. He would settle at the back with a clear view out the window. He never liked looking out the front window. Something about the oncoming traffic unnerved him. Today, he had managed to slip into the vehicle as they made their way to see the physician. Cassandra left a window partially open so Rex could fly in and out if he wanted to, and today, he did. But there was trouble brewing.

In some places, crows are territorial. When a younger male challenged him, a fight ensued. With all the scraps from the table, Rex had grown into a very large bird, quite larger, in fact, than most of the natives. When some of the other crows saw their buddy getting the worst of it, they also joined in attacking Rex. Two or three against one was not fair. He managed to get a few good pecks on all three of his opponents though, causing feathers to fly in all directions before he retreated into the vehicle through the open window. He rested for several minutes, catching his breath.

They did several tests on the little girl and took samples

of her blood. Rather than send them off and wait, Nadra Betcher, the lab technician, did some basic testing right on the spot. They discovered that Amelia had a rare type of cancer that often went terminal. Had this discovery come too late? She was transported via ambulance to the Bozeman Health Cancer Center. Since Cassandra went with her daughter in the ambulance and they departed out the back of the building, Rex was left alone in the vehicle and did not see them go. Cassandra or Casey as Mike called her had a bad habit. She would always forget to take her keys out of the ignition. Amy would remind her many times to remove them.

"Your keys, Mother. Don't forget your keys." Rex waited all night for the two to return. When they did not show up by the next morning, he exited the window when his opponents were not watching. A rabbit had been struck by a vehicle several roads over, so they were occupied. He sat on the very branch he had knocked the younger male off from and appeared to be thinking. Finally, as the wheels turned in his head, he remembered.

"Keys," he cried. "Keys." He reentered the window, and working them back and forth, he finally got the keys out of the ignition. "Rex help," he cried again as he rose into the air and made his way back to the ranch with the keys in his beak. Someone needed to keep an eye on things while his little mistress was away. Inside, after hanging them on the rack, he found the container that contained one remaining piece of chocolate cake. He worked the cover off and feasted. He had to come back three times to finish it, but when he was done, he was satisfied, almost.

In the process, the cake pan and cover fell face down on the floor. There were several choice morsels trapped underneath he would not be able to get at try as he might. It is too bad Casey was not home to photograph him. There was a large clump of chocolate frosting on one side of the top of his head and several flecks of crumbs and frosting over his feathers. Over the next half hour as he preened himself, Rex was now and again rewarded with a sweet treat. After resting for a while, trying to let his body digest all that sugar, he exited the window and checked in on the goats. They were hungry. Goats though were always hungry. Being the observant bird that he was, he noticed a burlap bag of oats up on a shelf too high for the critters to get to. There was twine around one end. This he worked back and forth until a small stream of the sweet grains started to sift out to the ground. The goats were very pleased. "Rex eat," he cawed as they gathered around.

During the day, Amelia often took out the pin to open the gate to let the goats out into a larger pasture. It had been long enough since being there for some grass to grow back, so after removing the pin, the gate swung open just enough for the animals to squeeze through. They would usually graze there during the day while the kids played, bounding around like jumping jacks and return to the shelter around dusk. One of the girls would then go and close the gate and pin it shut. Usually, Casey or Amy would feed the youngest of them with bottles in a separate pen, but when they were with their mothers, they would help themselves to a tender nipple or two. In a separate pen overnight, the nannies could produce some milk for the morning.

Since the folks were away, the nannies would be milked naturally by their kids, and a surplus would not build up. There would be oats, grass, and of course, water from the spring crossing the corner of the pasture for them to drink. Everyone would be happy and cared for thanks to one intelligent bird, Rex. Back at the house, after trying again to get the cake under the pan and failing, he looked around for some other food to eat. He found a loaf of bread in a plastic bag, and upon opening it, he took his share of its contents. It was not as sweet as the cake though.

Casey called Henry and told him what they knew so far about Amelia's condition and asked if he would go to the clinic and drive her vehicle home. She told him the keys were in the ignition, and that he might need to look for Rex if he was not inside. She then asked if he would feed and water the goats.

"Give them a little bit of oats but not too much. You will find a bag up on the shelf. If the nannies are full, they will need to be milked. If you do not want to do this, you can let the kids run with them and they will take care of that for you. Enough grass has grown back in the pasture so you can let them out with their babies. They will go back to the shelter in the evening. Rex can pretty much fend for himself. Do not be surprised if he starts talking to you. He is developing quite a vocabulary. I am not leaving the side of my precious Amelia. She is going to need her mommy more than ever in the upcoming days. Once we get a report back, I can probably get away for a few minutes to go back to the ranch and check things out."

Henry responded with a lot of compassion. He loved that little girl ever so much as he loved his own. She was the happiest little person he had ever known. She never complained, was always helpful, and always brightened up the day no matter how dark or stormy it might be outside. The most precious thing about her was her smile. When she was pleased, she showed it from deep inside. The smile that graced her face was so beautiful, even the angels of heaven must be envious.

"Take care of my little sunshine, sis. Do not worry about a thing at the ranch. We will take care of it for you. Just get her all better quickly."

After getting home, he picked up his wife, and together, they drove to the clinic to get the vehicle. It was unlocked. In her haste, the troubled mother had left everything open. The keys were not in the ignition though, and there was no sign of Rex. He would usually come when his name was called. It did not matter if he was half a mile away. When he heard his name, he would drop everything and come flying. Not knowing what else to do, they decided to drive out to the ranch. Henry was surprised to say the least that two sets of keys were on the key rack. There were only two sets of keys. How in the world could that be? His wife, Susan, was equally surprised to see the upside-down cake pan on the floor with the cover. When Henry reached for the keys, this huge black bird fluttered over and rested on the back of a nearby chair.

"Keys, Rex help," he cried as he watched the man remove them. Beckoning for his wife, they left, returning to the hospital to retrieve the vehicle.

"I have never seen a crow that large. How do you think he got that big so quickly? Last time we were here, he was a baby bird."

Being always ready with a quick answer, Sue responded, "I think he ate the entire chocolate cake." They both laughed. Back at the ranch with the retrieved car, Henry was again surprised to see that some oats had been given to the goats. The pin had been removed to the pasture just as Casey had asked, and the babies were running somehow with their moms, so he was relieved that he would not have to endure the task of milking. After taking one last look around before leaving, the crow came by for a final word.

"Rex help, Rex help Ahmil." Quite satisfied with his accomplishments, he returned to the open window as the car drove out of the driveway.

"You sure did help, Rex. It looks like you took care of all the chores, even seeing that the keys were returned to the rack. We are hoping that your little friend gets well soon and comes back here where she belongs with you and her mom. Keep looking after things, okay? I expect not much escapes your sharp, beady eyes."

***

CHAPTER 2
Cancer

When Amelia woke up, she was in a strange place. As her eyes adjusted to the room around her, she saw some tubes hooked up to her arm. Being curious, she tried to lift her arm to get a closer look, but something was preventing that from happening. She had never been shackled before, and fear came over her. Her mom had told her never to talk to strangers if she were alone for they could be bad people who might try to hurt her. Had some bad person captured and tied her down? She tried to remember what happened.

Slowly the last of her conscious memories came into her benumbed brain. She remembered walking up the hill. She was going to the spring to get a drink of water. Though in prison, her dad had gotten her a life straw as a Christmas present. It was supposed to filter out all the little bugs that might be in the water. She would lay down on her belly close to the small pond and stretch the straw out as long as it would go then suck up the sweet, sweet water. Rex would always land on a rock sticking out the middle of the pond and drink also. "Rex!" Where was her pet? She struggled hard against the restraints, but they would hardly budge. She was also very weak. What had happened?

There were some strange monitors in the room. One showed a series of jagged lines going up and down. When she struggled against the bands, she noticed the jagged lines grew taller. Besides the tubes coming out of her arm, there was something stuck in her mouth. Try as she might, she could not spit it out. Some type of cool, moist air was being fed into her mouth with a bit of mist mixed in. It was almost like going to the dentist when he was checking out her teeth. She had been in a hospital once before when her cousin was sick. She and her mom went to visit him there. Finally, it dawned on her. She had not been captured by some bad person but was in the hospital.

After struggling with her bounds for several minutes,

the little girl was finally able to free her left hand—the one that did not have the needle in it. She first used it to remove the contraption out of her mouth. Then she removed the tape that was attached to her right arm and pulled the needle out. A small stream of blood started seeping over her arm, but she was oblivious to it and loosened the strap that was holding that arm to the bed. She was free at last!

Amelia threw the covers back that were over her feet. She was dressed in a white robe. There was some uncomfortable thing between her legs. She pulled on it, and a stream of light yellow liquid dirtied the sheets. Amy wiggled her toes to be sure they were working. The remains of some red nail polish showed on six out of ten of them. She would have her mother fix them as soon as she got home. She had to find Rex. By now, he would be worried sick over her. Her legs came over the edge of the bed, and she let them slowly down to the floor. When she tried to stand up though, they would not support her weight. She fell forward, hitting her head on the corner of the table. Blood started coming out of a wound it caused as well as the small amount that was still coming out of the hole in her arm where the needle had been. Everything went black. She had no idea the hospital had placed her on blood thinners.

***

Cassandra had refused to leave the side of her little girl for days. When she was tired, she would go to the little bench by the window and catch a few minutes of troubled sleep. The news that came back from the many tests was not good. Her daughter had two types of cancer ravaging her little body. The one that caused her to black out up by the spring was a brain tumor. It was growing at an alarming rate. It was in a place where if they were to attempt to remove it, her beautiful face with that sweet, sweet smile would be scarred forever. The little mother was very distressed. It was at times like these she needed the strong arms of her husband to surround and comfort her, but they were rotting away in a prison cell. The other problem Amelia was facing was the second type of cancer. They had diagnosed it as a Wilms tumor. Wilms tumors are a type of kidney cancer that develop from cells

20

called nephroblasts. It is also called nephroblastomas. Dr. Max Wilms wrote the first medical paper about this condition, and that was how it got its name.

Kidney cancer in children is rare, but Wilms tumor is the most common type. Almost one hundred children between the ages of zero and fourteen years are diagnosed with Wilms tumor each year in the US. They are most common in children under five. They rarely develop in older children and almost never in adults.

Wilms tumors usually only affect one kidney (unilateral). But in fewer than ten out of one hundred children, it can affect both kidneys (bilaterial). Amelia had it in both kidneys. With two types of cancer battling for dominance in her precious little girl, her chances of recovery were very slim. Besides all the things that were going on in the life of this single mom, she now had to figure out a way to tell her little one she was probably going to die. How do you tell a child they will probably die? How do you describe to them what death is all about? Amelia had been comatose for two weeks. No one could give this distraught mother any hope of her ever-regaining consciousness. Finally, after being beside her daughter for days without end it seemed, Cassandra had slipped away to look on things at the ranch.

Rex came flying frantically up to the SUV, and before it even stopped, he had fluttered around to each window, looking for his mistress. As Cassandra applied the brakes and turned off the key, he landed on the hood and peered in at her through the windshield. When the door opened, he hopped to the top of it and cried out, "Ahmil, Ahmil? Rex help Ahmil?"

If birds can look sad, Rex looked very sad as he saw the empty car seat at the back. He flew to it and pecked on the top, as if his attempt would cause the little girl to emerge. He did it half a dozen times and finally cried in his most distressed tone, "Ahmil, gone?"

The little mother's heart was further wrenched by the sadness expressed by her daughter's pet. How do you express to a bird that he might never again see the one he loved most and best in all the world, Ahmil? As Cassandra headed up the stairs to her house, he lighted on her shoulder. She could feel the nails of his feet digging into it. Amelia had learned this long before and usually wore a piece of leather attached to her underarm on the shoulder he perched on.

Once inside, he flew to his normal perch and settled down to cleaning some dead skin off his feet. He appeared to Cassandra to have grown even larger than she remembered in the two plus weeks she had been absent.

After grabbing a bite to eat and giving Rex some of his favorite treats, Cassandra headed up to the barn to check on the goats. It had been a couple of weeks since they had been milked. Hopefully, the kids were seeing to their mothers needs. Looking around, she saw that the grass had grown exceptionally tall along the road to the barn. Perhaps she could place some cables on the nannies and tie them off at twenty-inch intervals. They would clean away the grass better than any weed whacker in a little while. All of her girls came over to get some much-needed love and affection as she entered the pen.

Casey bent to examine the tits of her prize goat. They were in rough shape. A scratch had gone down one side and was infected. The lady went over and grabbed a cloth and ran it under water until it was hot and steaming. She carefully bathed the wound, allowing the moisture to soften some of the scabs. After a little bit, she took down some iodine and generously worked it into the scrape. Beth Ann stomped her back foot a little but held her ground. After it was saturated, some Bag Balm was placed over it. Soon, things would be okay, but the scar would prevent her Beth from ever being in another show. Usually on the show goats, they never let the kids nurse them, especially as they grew larger like these were.

"No more shows for you, girl," the farmer's wife stated as she gave the girl another hug for good measure. But what did shows matter now anyway with her little one wasting away in her special room? Overwhelmed with grief, the little mother closed the gate behind her and headed up to the spring. This is where she would go when things got too hard to bear.

There was something special about the place that was sacred. Just the idea of pure, clean water coming out of the hillside was a wonder in itself, and the water was so clear. Was there a balm somewhere in Gilead to make the wounded whole? Rex joined her, flying slowly just above in the sky as she hiked up the hill. Upon arriving, he flew down to the very spot where Amelia had been lying so still on the ground. Landing lightly there, he cawed out his special name for her, "Ahmil!"

It is hard to say how long she sat by the spring. She

22

was praying as only a mother can pray. High in the heavens, looking down on this distraught child of the kingdom, the great Creator of all decided to send her a sign. Cassandra had her eyes closed for a long time as she pleaded with God for the life of her child. When she opened them, a doe had joined her there across the spring. She had a young fawn by her side. As the little mother looked deep into the doe's lovely brown eyes, an assurance of peace came over her. There was love in those eyes.

Perhaps Amelia's angel had taken up residence there for a short time and was looking out at this woman. As if to add more assurance, the little fawn shook her head up and down to agree with whatever thoughts were communicated between the two at that moment.

"Thank you, Lord Jesus. I now know that you have heard my prayer, and whatever happens in the future, it is in Your hands now. There is nothing more I can do, so it is up to You. Thank You again. Amen."

Rex beat her back to the barn. He entered the area where the oats were kept and opened the sack a little so some of them fell down on the barn floor. He then lifted the opening back up on the shelf. When Cassandra entered, he cried out to her, "Rex help, Rex help Ahmil!" He then took to the sky.

Cassandra watched as he flew up to the log cabin and settled on a branch above where Joyce was burning some papers. One letter was giving her a hard time. Whenever she attempted to throw it in the fire, a gust of wind would come and move it away from the flames. She would go around and pick it up to try and burn it again, but another gust of wind would move it just out of reach. She was getting a bit agitated. At last, a corner of it caught fire, and she breathed a sigh of relief. Just as it was about to burst completely into flames, a large bird swooped down from apparently out of nowhere and scooped it up in his beak. A gust of wind came causing the fire to flare up for a second. It singed some of the smaller feathers on his face before the flame was extinguished.

The former secretary lunged at the bird, but it was too late. He was up, up and away. She looked around for something to try and knock him out of the air. A large stick came flying in his direction but fell far short of its mark. He entered the house through his usual window and placed the partially burned letter with some of the many trinkets he had managed to collect over his lifetime. Perhaps it was the gold-colored stamp on the green envelope that attracted his attention. It has been said that beauty is in the eyes of the beholder. Perhaps that was true, but then again, this was not unusual for Rex. He has a special liking for shiny things.

At that precise moment, Cassandra received a call from the cancer center. There had been an accident. Supposedly, the little girl had finally awakened and somehow managed to free herself before falling face first, hitting her head on the corner of a stand. The mother rushed as fast as her short legs would carry her to the vehicle. As she sped out of the driveway, Rex somehow managed to fly in through one of the open windows.

"Rex, you get out of here. You can't come with me. They only allow approved pets that have been highly trained into the building to help some of the children deal with their trauma." She swatted at the creature, but he settled down in the car seat of his beloved mistress. He looked so determined, and she did not have the heart to drive him away. "Okay!" she cried out in frustration as she over corrected at the steering wheel. The vehicle swerved sharply toward the side of the road, but in the nick of time, she managed to get it going straight again. "You might as well come along now that you are here, but you must stay in the vehicle. Amelia fell and hurt herself badly."

***

CHAPTER 3
The Recurring Dream

Amelia kept having a reoccurring dream. In each one, she was at the spring looking up at the top of the mountain that marked the end of their property. She would struggle to get up from the ground. When that did not work, she would crawl forward, putting her arms ahead of her knees. She would keep crawling until she got to the path, and once there, she would try without success to get up on her feet again. She did not have the strength to do that, so she would crawl a little further up the path and try to stand up again. Each time she fell, she would look up to the top of the mountain. There was something very shiny up there. It looked beautiful.

In her heart of hearts, Amelia knew if she could just get to the shiny thing, everything would be alright. She was so determined to reach it that she decided if she must crawl all the way up there, she would do it, and if she came to the place where she couldn't crawl anymore, she would pull herself forward on her belly—if necessary, with her arms and feet. She had to accomplish this task, or she felt like something bad would happen from which there was no return. If she woke up and went back to sleep, the dream would start out at the spring again. She would do it all over, except each time she dreamed and woke up, she was further up the mountain than before.

Nadra Betcher was so moved by Amelia's condition that she decided to study Wilms tumor research as much as possible. If there was a successful treatment or cure anywhere in the world, she would find it. She would move mountains to save that beautiful little girl's life. She found that when a baby is growing in the womb, the kidneys develop very early on, but sometimes something goes wrong. This can cause some of the early (immature) cells (or nephroblasts) to not turn into developed (mature) kidney cells. If this happens, they begin to grow out of control and may develop into a cancer known as a Wilms tumor.

On her way to the hospital, Cassandra got a call on her

cell phone. It was a number she did not recognize, but with the condition of her little girl, any call might be important, so she answered it.

"Hello, this is Nadra Betcher. You may not remember me, but I was the one who took the first samples of Amelia's blood when you brought her in. I understand she was diagnosed with Wilms tumor. Is that correct?"

Casey pondered the question for a few seconds before answering, "Yes, that is my understanding. It usually only affects one kidney, but Amelia has it in both, plus the brain tumor is keeping her from being conscious. I stayed by her side day and night, but wouldn't you know it, the first time I leave to check things out at home, she wakes up. I was not there to tell her anything. My poor little girl must have been scared to death to wake up in a strange place with no one around she knew. Did you hear she unhooked herself from all the tubes, even the restraints and tried to walk?"

"No, I did not know that. What happened? She must be very weak."

"She was or must have been. They said she fell and hit her head on a stand and got a deep gash on her face. She was also knocked unconscious again. My poor little girl was all alone there. I will never forgive myself for leaving."

"I am so sorry, Cassandra. It must be very difficult to be going through this all alone. Could you answer a question or two?"

The call was coming through Cassandra's radio. Above her head was a little microphone. An Amber Alert came on and drowned out the voice of the nurse. After it was over, the conversation continued, "What is it you would like to know?"

Nadra shuffled some papers in front of her to help organize her thoughts before talking. "Did Amelia have a troubled birth?"

Cassandra was thinking about it. It all flashed back. Was the birth process traumatic for Amelia? She had never thought of what the baby might have gone through to come into the world. She certainly remembered what she went through. "I guess I never thought of what it must have been like for Amelia. She needed to be partially pushed back in and turned. Then they had to cut on me a little to make the opening big enough for her to come out. So yes, I expect you could say she had a troubled birth."

26

The nurse looked at her papers again then continued, "The trouble she went through in her birth probably contributed to the cancer that has taken control of her kidneys. I do not know what would cause the tumor in her brain. I am researching this on my own time. I want to help. Can I call you at times, and can you call me with updates? I may be on a dry path, but there was a case of another little girl in the EU that had a similar condition, and she is now on the road to complete recovery. They did something with peptides, using a host body to manufacture a strain of T cells that caused the cancer tumors to shrink. If there is even a little chance for your daughter, I would like to help. The treatments they used on Sandy, the girl in the EU, are not the ones practiced at Bozeman Health Cancer Center."

Cassandra did not know if she wanted to trust the life Amelia into the hands of Nadra or not. She did not even know if she trusted the people who were even now in control of her precious life. What do you do in cases like this? There are hundreds of supposed cures for cancer out there. A lot of them are pure quackery. "Yes, I will keep you updated, Nadra, on Amelia's progress, be it for better or worse. I want my little girl back again all happy and healthy more than anything else in the world. You have to know that. I might be willing to look at your research sometime in the future. You have my number. If she takes a turn for the worst, I will give you a call."

"That is all I am asking, Cassandra. I too want Amelia to be perfectly healthy and back home with you again."

Just then, the big black bird decided to add his two cents to the conversation. "Rex help Ahmil, Rex help."

"Does Amelia have a pet parakeet?" the nurse asked as she heard the comment. It sounded far away, like the bird was in a cage or something.

"No, it is just Rex, her pet crow."

The Amber Alert blared out again, and the connection with Nadra was lost.

***

When Cassandra arrived at the hospital, they ushered her into Amelia's room. The little girl was whiter than her mother had ever seen her. They had shaved off all her hair.

A large bandage was wrapped around one side of her head. It even covered one eye. She was so still. For the first time in her life, the little mother realized that the chances Amelia was going to die were very good. It was the most terrifying thought she ever had. How could she go back to the world without her precious little daughter? She started sobbing uncontrollably. A nurse brought her a chair and a soft dry cloth as the tears spilled down her face. Finally, she spoke, "What happened?"

Her doctor entered the room, so the nurse turned the question over to him. "Amelia woke up and unbound herself. I do not know how she worked her arm loose, but she did and unhooked everything. She then tried to get up and walk, but her legs would not support her. So she fell face first into a stand. She struck her head in the exact spot the tumor was growing inside and got a gash there. It was very deep. We were able to go through her skull and take a sample of the cancerous tissue before closing the wound. The biopsy is over in our laboratory right now being analyzed. Your little girl helped us a lot."

"Is she going to be alright?" The frantic mother did not want to hear about all the advances they were making in her case at this moment. She wanted to know about her girl.

"Actually, Amelia is doing very well considering what happened. Once she heals up, the scar will be mostly covered by her eyebrow. She is very fortunate."

This soothed the distraught mother a little, and she took the cloth and dried up her face where the tears had dampened it. She then patted each eye to dry them. About that time, there was a lot of commotion in the hallway. Cassandra saw a man dressed in light blue garb with a broom in hand. He was chasing a large black bird. She jumped up from the chair and ran out of the door, hollering at him.

"Stop! Stop! Don't hurt him. He is Amelia's pet crow. She raised him from a baby. Please stop chasing him."

The surprised man lowered the broom, and Rex, realizing that the airways were finally clear, came and landed on Casey's shoulder. "Rex here. Rex help Ahmil."

People all up and down the hallway looked on in wonder. This was clearly the largest crow any of them had ever seen and to think that not only was it tamed, but it could also talk. The little mother and the crow re-entered the room where Amelia was lying. When he saw his little mistress, he hopped off the shoulder of the lady and landed on the bed next to his beloved. "Ahmil? Ahmil? Ahmil sleep?"

Rex turned his head and looked at the surprised people that had gathered at the door to observe this unusual reunion. He went over to the little girl, and reaching down gently, he took her one exposed ear lobe in his beak.

Amelia made a low mummer then opened her eyes. There, looking down at her was her precious pet. In a very weak voice, she spoke, "Rex, you came to help me. I love you." Then she closed her eyes again and continued with her dream.

She had gotten further up the mountain toward the shiny thing than ever before. But it cost her. She could no longer crawl. She was inching herself forward, little by little on her tummy. The rough rocks and sticks were digging into her skin. Her knuckles and feet were scratched and bruised. That was when she saw Rex. He came flying toward her and landed right in front of her. In her dream, she heard him talking. When she looked up, the shiny thing was advancing down the mountain path toward her. It was beautiful.

The little girl smiled her sweetest smile, and so she did. Everyone in the hospital room saw it, it was the most beautiful smile that any little girl had ever smiled before because Amelia's smile came from all the way down in her heart all the way up to her face.

***

CHAPTER 4
A Dad's Prayer

Mike had precious little time with his daughter during her six years of life all thanks to a wrongful conviction of the death of his manager. When the prison was informed of the state of Amelia's health, arrangements were made for him to go and visit her. He would be escorted by officers, of course, but since it looked like the little girl's life was hanging in the balance, there were some with compassion that felt he could do this. He had been a model prisoner during his stay there.

Prior to this conviction, he had no criminal records of any kind. More than one person felt he had been wrongfully convicted in the first place, but based on lack of further evidence, he had been sentenced. Judge Danny Thompson seemed to have had a vendetta against him from the first day of the trial. Mike and Danny had gone to the same grade school. Danny had been small for his age and was the recipient of a lot of bullying. Mike, on the other hand, had always been tall for his age, and no one ever had picked on him. In fact, during his elementary school years, he had never once gotten into a fight with another person. Add to that his good looks, and perhaps Danny, remembering those school days, let it affect his judgment.

Once Danny gained the status of judge, some would argue he wanted to get even with certain people for the pain he had suffered, especially good-looking and successful people. The judge was still short, and he was bald. His forehead was small, and his nose overly large. He would not have won any beauty contests. Judge Thompson had given Mike the worst conviction possible, short of execution. On his visit, Cassandra was forbidden to see him. It was some crazy rule that Dan had added to the terms of his conviction.

At the hospital, he was led into the room of his little girl. She appeared as still as death itself to him. The head wound had healed, so the bandages were no longer there. But she still had a blackened eye below the scar. This father's heart of love went out to his precious daughter. He sat down beside her, occasionally kissing her forehead. She had not awakened since Rex entered the room so unexpectedly. That had been nearly three days ago now. Nothing they did seemed to rouse her. They considered her comatose. The results of the last scan showed the tumor had increased in size and was the probable reason for this.

Mike sat there for a long time. During the thirty years of his life, he had not been particularly religious. His parents and grandparents had never taken him to church. The few times he had entered one was either for a funeral or a wedding. His concept of God was this being up there who got upset with humans when they misbehaved and reprimanded them, making them feel guilty for their wrongdoings. The idea of a God of love was foreign to him.

Now, however, as he saw his precious child so helpless, the first part of the Lord's Prayer came into his mind. "Our Father which art in heaven." Was not God a father? Yes. He had a son who the Bible called Jesus. Would a father wish this sickness on anyone? Not a normal father. He knew he himself would never wish such suffering on any of his children. Perhaps the Father in heaven loved His children even as Mike loved his child Amelia. These were new thoughts. He bowed his head and let the words that were forming in his mind go upward. He imagined a kind, loving father up there looking down at him even as he was looking down at his daughter.

"Heavenly Father, I have been told that you are a God of love. Right now, I might even have felt that. But what kind of a God would allow this to happen to my precious daughter? You are a Father. I am told You had a Son, but you stood by and let Your Son die. You could have stopped it from happening, but you didn't. Are You going to stand by and do nothing also with Amelia?" Bitterness came boiling to the surface of his mind. He grew angrier with each thought.

"Have a heart, Father, or are you even worthy of such a name? Where is your love now? My little girl did nothing to deserve this kind of treatment. I have done some bad things. I admit that. I tried to tell myself my false conviction was a result of some bad things I did back when I was a foolish teenager. But my sweet, sweet Amelia has done nothing wrong. She is as sweet as an angel. She has never been a problem like I was but always cooperated with her mom. So I am appealing to You now. If you are what the Bible says You are, prove it to me. Do something to reverse this cancer in the sweetest little girl that was ever born. Please, Dear God. If You will not or cannot do anything for her, how can her mother and I expect the doctors to have any better success? Finally, if this sickness is because of something I did bad or something her mother might have done in the past, forgive us. We want our little girl back. Bring her back from this terrible position she is in. Amen."

After finishing his prayer, Mike took Amelia's little hands in his own and spoke softly to her, "Amelia, your daddy is here to see you. They told me I needed to come because you are not feeling very good. I am here. I would have been here a lot more if they let me. I love you so much. I missed so much of your life—you're growing up, your adventures with Rex, and a thousand other things. Sweetheart, I love you more than life itself. If it would help you get better, I would do anything, go anywhere. They told me we have the same blood type. If you had a different sickness and needed any organ I have in my body, I would gladly give it to you so you could be normal, but you got the wrong kind of sickness. I love you so much. I have always loved you and always will. I love your smile. It is so sweet it makes the birds sing. I love your momma too more than she can ever know and would have liked nothing better than to raise you with her like normal moms and dads do. Oh sweetheart, if I could live these last seven years over, I would do so many things differently."

From somewhere in the distance, his tender words registered in the compressed brain of his little girl. Amelia opened her eyes and looked right at him then spoke, "Daddy, you have come too. Now all we need is Momma, and everything will be better. Could you hold me, Daddy? I want you to hold me without any of these tubes. Could the nurse come and take them out while you hold me? If you could hold me for just a little while, I would like that better than anything else in the world."

One of the officers nodded as Mike gave him a look. He had heard the request of the little girl and went and got a nurse. In a short time, the task was done, and Mike was able to lift his little girl out of the bed. He carried her in his arms to a large reclining chair and sat down. In all his life, he had only been able to hold her one other time back when she was a little baby. It was wonderful to do it again. After getting settled, she rewarded him with one of her sweet smiles. "Can I kiss you, Daddy? I have wanted to kiss you for such a long, long time."

"You certainly can, Amelia. I would love that." Some salty tears flowed down his cheeks as he lowered his head down toward her face. Her kiss was soft and sweet. She did it three times, and when finished, she gave him even a sweeter smile. Then she went back to sleep while secure in his arms. In her dream, her daddy had come and picked her up in his arms. She had pointed him to the shiny thing. When he looked at it, he could see it was an angel. The angel stopped its downward movement and stood silently, waiting for Mike and the little girl to come toward him. The path was steep. Normally, that would have been no problem for this once powerful man, but years in a prison cell and not much chance for exercise had weakened him. He labored with her in his arms up the steep path.

Back in the hospital, Mike's allotted time to visit his daughter was up. He had to go back with those accompanying him. He stood and kissed his daughter one more time before gently laying her back on the bed. The nurse reattached the tubes. Looking back one more time, he saw her there, but she did not appear so white and still. There was a lot more color in her face. She was asleep again, holding her last smile. The love-starved father took a mental picture of that smile. He would hold unto it forever if possible. Perhaps by holding unto it, the healing both of them needed would come at last.

Cassandra was coming in his direction as he was leaving. He knew he had to give her a hug. She was running toward his open arms when the officers intercepted her. Mike could not contain himself any longer. He had to do it.

"Officer, what harm would come if I hugged my wife? Tell me."

The officer was quick to respond, "Nothing, Mike, but it is forbidden."

"Why? What have I done so terrible that makes it so I cannot hold my wife?"

"I do not know, Mike. There were rules set in your conviction, and I am following those rules."

"Please. I have not held her for six years."

The officer turned his back. So did the other one. One looked north and the other south.

Mike and Cassandra embraced for a long time. They

wept together. Tears streamed down both of their faces. Six years of pain and agony came to the surface of each. Then the giant gave her one last kiss on her forehead and made his way to the first officer.

As they exited the building, wanting to make sure no word of this got out, Rodney spoke, "I didn't see anything back there, did you Paul?"

"Nope," came the reply. "I didn't see a thing."

***

Back in her dream, Amelia felt her daddy placing her in the strong arms of her angel. For the first time, she looked into his face. She reached up and traced it with her free hand. He was so beautiful, and he was smiling. She instantly fell in love with him. After a while, she started talking to him and wonder of wonders, he responded.

"What is your name, angel," the little girl asked as she looked deep into his eyes. They were clear and bright and filled with light.

His face shone with a shimmering radiance. He truly was very good-looking, almost as good-looking as her daddy.

"What do you want my name to be, Amelia?"

"I do not know. Maybe something that means kindness. You are so kind to hold me in your arms like this and talk to me."

"I have a long name, Amelia, but you can call me Ademar. It means 'one who is popular for his kindness.' I have been waiting for both your mom and dad to bring you to me. Your mom prayed for this last week right over there by the spring, and then when your daddy prayed also, it was enough. We can be together now. Do you have any questions you wish to ask me?"

The little girl thought for a few seconds, trying to form in her mind this first question. Finally, she spoke, "What happened to me, Ademar? Suddenly, I got very tired, then things went dark all around me."

The angel looked at her with a soft, kind expression as he answered, "You have a bad disease called cancer. The reason it is so bad is that some of your cells have rebelled against the rest of your body and have started growing in ways they are

34

not supposed to grow. They are not obeying the instruction your body has given."

Ademar carried Amelia up to the very top of the mountain. The view there was beautiful. The two of them could look out over the mountains and valleys. Groups of clouds, looking like fluffy popcorn, hung in the sky, and a wonderful breeze was blowing. She had been laboring so hard to get to the shiny thing that there was sweat over much of her body. The cool breeze dried it.

The angel continued speaking, "You have this disease in three places. There is a large group of these rebellious cells growing in your head, doing things they shouldn't—kind of like the baby goats that do not like to obey their mommies. They go places and do things they are not supposed to do. You also have cells doing things down in the organs called kidneys. Do you have much pain in your body, Amelia?"

"Not a lot in my head. In my head, it feels like there is something big there that does not belong. Sometimes I get headaches. The worst problem is I cannot see very good out of my right eye. There is something that makes that eye see darker. I do hurt when I have to go number 1. Sometimes it hurts so bad I want to cry. In the hospital, they put something down there, and it does not hurt so bad. I have heard that angels can do miracles. Could you make my head and eyes feel better?"

"I could make your head feel better," Ademar responded as he stroked her bald head with one of his hands while looking into her bad eye. "If I made it feel better though and took the bad thing with its darkness away, you would no longer be able to see me. The reason you can see me is because it is there. Would you like me to make it feel better?"

"Yes, but if it will make you go away, what would happen if I kept it there like it is?"

"You would eventually die."

"What happens when I die?" The little girl had seen dead things. Rex had nearly died. One of the momma goats died while giving birth to twins. Amelia had seen her all cold and stiff. Her beautiful eyes dried up and shriveled.

"When you die, honey, it is like going to sleep at night. You do not know anything that happens all night long."

"If I were to die tonight, would I see you in the morning when I wake up?"

"Yes, I would be the first person you see. Then I would take you to your mommy and daddy."

"Would Daddy not be in prison in the morning when you took me to them?"

"No, your daddy would not be in prison. He would be with your mommy. You would be with them forever. All of you would be together forever."

"Would Rex be there in the morning with Mommy and Daddy?"

"If Jesus wanted him to be there, he would be there."

Then the little girl asked a question that made the angel quite sad. Jesus had not been part of their family like He is part of a lot of families in the world. "Who is Jesus?"

***

CHAPTER 5
The Letter

Henry was at the ranch doing the chores one day when he found Rex's stash of collectables. There were several shiny trinkets he had collected along with some wrappers of candy bars and shiny dimes. There was one shiny quarter among the items also. When he saw the letter, he was curious. It was burned around the edges, but the gold stamp appeared to be untouched. He decided it was the stamp that had caught the bird's attention. It was gold around the edges and had a golden daisy on it with the word LOVE at the bottom.

The most unusual aspect of the letter though was who it was addressed to. It was Mike's former secretary. Should he read it? Rex might be the only one who complained if he knew, but he had not followed Henry into the house. The return address had no name, only an address—an address that jogged something in his mind. He typically would never read another person's mail, but since he thought he knew both of the parties and they were of interest to Mike's imprisonment, why not? He pulled the contents from the envelope, wiping some of the charred colorant from his hand before reading.

"My Dearest Joyce:"

I am so excited that you and Paul are finalizing your divorce papers. What he did to you at that swinger party was disgusting. He lied to you by saying that it was a few friends getting together for a barbeque and some drinks. You had no idea that once you all had drunk enough to dull your senses, that you all would be swapping partners for sex. It turns my stomach. No wonder you were furious with him once you found out the real purpose of the party. What he did to you on the diving board was absolutely crazy! I would never treat you that way if we had a million years together. It was so embarrassing for you. I can't even imagine how you were feeling after a stunt like that. Then when the other men there started whistling and calling out your name, making remarks about the now exposed personal parts of your body? What is this world coming to? I do not know how you had the presence of mind after a dastardly deed like that to collect your things and run from the place. We both have Judge Thompson to thank since he happened to be passing by at the exact time you reached the road to give you a ride. What if it had been someone you didn't know, someone who would have hurt you? It is good that Mike gave you those hotel vouchers so that when Paul got back to your place, you were not around. No telling what he would have done to you. You hurt his pride in front of his buddies. If he ever struck you, sweetheart I think I would kill him.

So here is the good news! I am scheduled to go to Vegas this weekend. I found out by way of the grapevine that Paul will also be there, taking in a convention in a different part of the city. I am going to confront him and tell him what I think of him. I suppose one would call it giving a person hell. That is what he has coming and what he will get from me. I am usually a quiet type of person, but when I see injustice done, especially to the one I love dearest and best, I cannot keep silent. I am going to let him know what you told me about all of this and why he is a dirty jerk.

I have waited all my life for someone as sweet and lovely as you. I fell in love with you back at college the very first time I saw you. You were with Jill. When Paul hooked up with you, I wanted to punch him out. I knew what type of guy he was and tried to get some time with you to let you know he was all show. It never worked out, not until you became the secretary. When you applied, it was my recommendation that got you the job and with a salary higher than he was paying Peggy, his former secretary. I am so glad you came to work here and that you have decided to be mine. I feel like the luckiest man alive now. Remember this, I will always love you and never treat you bad like Paul has done. Am counting the days until we can tie the knot forever. You probably will need to stay at my place for a while until the lawyers work out the details of your divorce. I am sure they will award the log home to you. They usually give the house to the wife. After a few weeks, when Paul is forever gone from your world, then we might *look at moving back into your place. It is a little nicer than mine, although mine is a lot closer to work. In fact, we could walk to work together, be there in ten, twelve minutes if we had to. Actually, that might be nice. I would love to have you hanging on my arm some bright, crisp morning as we walked to work. I love you so much it hurts every minute we are apart. I just wanted to get this off my chest and let you know I am excited to start our new life together.*

Loving you always and then more and more. You're the best friend I have ever had.

"Your forever soulmate, Jim"

Henry placed the letter back in the envelope and looked around for a place to stash it. He needed to show this to Cassandra. It is a crying shame this letter had not been presented as evidence during Mike's court trial. Had they had it, he might never have gone to jail. This was proof that Joyce and Jim were having an affair, and that Jim somehow let Joyce convince him that she was going to divorce Paul and marry him. It had never happened. Last he knew, she and Paul were still together. They had never divorced. If she had not stopped Jim from going to Las Vegas, which was the only way she knew how, he would have confronted Paul and then he would have known she was cheating on him with Jim. She couldn't have that. She wanted to keep her cake and eat it too. So she conjured up a story about him as an excuse to keep Jim where she wanted him, wrapped around her little finger.

There was a problem though. Once a trial happened and a person was convicted, there was only a little while for an appeal to be made. That time had long passed. If this evidence was presented and the dates worked out with Jim's murder, the best Mike could hope for was a reduced sentence. That would need to be appealed and go through a bunch of red tape. They would probably haul Joyce back and who knows by now what excuse she would come up with. Plus, the letter was a personal one. It showed intent, but was it enough? Probably not. The question would also come up as to how this letter from some six years ago would end up in their hands in the first place. Can you imagine them hearing that a crow brought the letter right into Cassandra's house and practically handed it to her? They would not believe it. Then how did a bird of all things come to get the letter in the first place? They might have to bring the crow in to testify. That would be fun!

Henry decided to place the letter in the antique desk that belonged to Mike's grandmother. He headed for it, but before he had a chance to stop him, Rex swooped down and grabbed it out of his hand. He was a quick one, that bird was! In a flash, he was through the open window. He looked at Henry from a branch outside and called out with the letter still in his beak. His words were muffled a bit but still audible enough to be understood.

"Miiine, miine and Ahmil's." With that, he was up, up, and away. Henry ran out the door and watched where he went. Rex flew to a large pine tree halfway up the mountain. There appeared to be a large nest there. So Rex has found himself a pretty woman. Is he raising a family? Will the babies rip the evidence to shreds? Going back into the house, Henry got out some powerful binoculars and looked. There were babies in the nest, and a Mrs. Rex did not give the letter to them. Instead, he wedged it between the nest and a branch. If only Amelia was here. She was probably the only one who can get him to bring it back.

***

Nadra Betcher received the papers she sent in the mail. The author had not placed them on the internet because he did not want to take the chance of being censored or his work being jeopardized before he had a chance to fully develop it. He claimed that every person has within their body the means to cure any kind of disease they may encounter, including cancer. Some fluids would need to be removed from the sick person and purified, perhaps using some biological organism or organism's circulatory system. Several cancer patients had been treated successfully through these means. Some even had stage 4 cancer and made a complete recovery. The same day she received his papers, a kit arrived from the EU that could test Amelia's blood and pinpoint exactly what types of cancer made up the tumor in her brain. It was amazing what this test could do!

The test worked analyzing a type of DNA released by the tumor cells. They shed into the blood what is known as cell-free DNA (cfDNA). The challenge came when those analyzing

40

the results tried to identify the tumor-specific cfDNA because many other cells also released DNA into the blood. This test, however, detected DNA that was specifically from cancer cells using changes to the DNA, namely the addition of a chemical from a methyl group in the body that was associated within the tumor growth. After isolating the cfDNA from the blood sample and sequencing it to find the methylated parts, healthcare professionals could feed the results into a computer program able to isolate and recognize DNA from cancer and noncancer cells. The test could also look at the various proteins within the person and analyze if there was an imbalance in some portion of their body. Protein concentrations in the tissue around tumors was quite a bit different than in other areas of the body that were noncancerous.

This process was tested on some four thousand people, half of whom had cancer and came out with a 93 percent accuracy. There was some of Amelia's blood at the clinic. Nadra could run the test on it if she found some way to get her hands on it. If she got caught stealing some of the blood for her own purposes, it could cost her job. This was strictly forbidden. But was it worth the risk? What if between the research of the doctor and the test that would positively identify the exact cancer growing in this little girl's body, she could be cured completely? Yes, if this were to happen, Nadra would gladly say goodbye to her job. Was this not what people in the medical field were pledging their lives to?

***

After receiving the letter from Jim, murdering him, and pinning the blame on her boss, Joyce decided divorcing her husband was far too suspicious at that time. Over the next few months and years, she went out of her way to show him she appeared to still be his lovely bride. She did special little things for Paul and went out of her way to be nice. He came running back to her only too glad to not have to divide up their possessions. They took a long vacation to Europe, they went on cruises to Alaska and the Caribbean, and they even took one in Hawaii. It was like they were kids in love all over again. She played him like a fiddle.

Joyce was so diabolical that this act was kept up for

nearly six years. Then she hit him with everything she could throw at him. She hired the services of the best divorce lawyer in the state. Paul could not believe it when he was served the papers. So far, as he was concerned, they were both still madly in love with each other. The last few years had been wonderful! He was sure he had the sweetest wife in Montana. It completely threw him for a loop. She got almost everything. He was left with his truck, a fifth wheel, and only a small portion of their savings.

Joyce decided to sell the house and get out of state. It was best to leave this place behind forever. The day she put the home on the market was the same day Henry found the letter. Over the next several days, he got very little sleep. He was kept awake trying to figure out how to recover the letter from the crow's nest. He had to keep the interest of Amelia in mind above all else. Rex was her best friend in the entire world. He had been to her room more than once. Each time Rex came and took her ear lobe in his beak, she woke up and talked to him. She told him about her dream as if he were aware of every detail of it. He and her daddy had come at just the right time.

It was during one of her conversations with Rex that those listening heard for the first time about her angel. Of course, she knew that Rex knew about her angel. She knew that her daddy knew about her angel, even though he didn't and couldn't because of his imprisonment. It was during one of these visits with Rex that Henry, listening in from the other side of the room, found out that a windstorm had come and knocked a letter out of the tree. Amelia told Rex about it. The bird appeared to get upset and wanted to leave her quicker than normal. Was it possible he understood the word letter? Cassandra and Henry listened intently as she told him about it.

"Rex?"

"Yes, Ahmil."

"Do you remember the other day when it was so windy?"

"Windy?" The bird asked as he cocked his head from one side to the other. His black beady eyes were drilling into those of the little girl, trying to understand.

Amelia made a whooo sound with her mouth while waving her free hand in an up-and-down motion. Then she blew her breath as hard as she could in his face, letting the air escape as she phrased the word again, "Whiiinnndy." She did not have the strength to do it as long and hard as she wanted to.

"Windy, whiindy, windy." The words were hissed out of his mouth. Then he did a funny thing. He waved his wings up and down, putting out as much wind as he could with them just short of taking to the air. It fanned Amelia's face in the process.

"Yes, Rex! You got it. You are the smartest bird in the whole world." She gave another one of her smiles, the ones that came all the way down from somewhere inside and spread over her face like the morning sunshine spreads over the meadow. She continued speaking with the smile still there for all to see. "When the wind blew, a letter came flying down from your nest. It landed about ten feet from the spring. It had a gold stamp on it. My angel showed it to me. It is a LOVE stamp, Rex. The golden flower on the stamp is a daisy. My angel told me most daisies have an even number of petals on them, but the gold daisy on the stamp has an uneven number of petals. This is so when you pull the petals out one by one and say, 'he loves me or she loves me not, she loves me, he loves me not,' the gold daisy will end with 'he loves me,' not like the real-life daisy's that mostly end with 'he loves me not.'"

Henry did not know if he believed in angels or not, but he was about to find out. He slipped away so quietly that not even Cassandra or Rex saw him go. He beat it to his truck and nearly got a speeding ticket going to the ranch. Some little voice in his head said, Slow down, Henry, just before he came to the bottom of the hill. He did, and though he was still going some six miles per hour faster than the limit, he only got a side long glance of disapproval from the officer behind the wheel as he passed.

There was a road that went all the way up to the spring. He drove there with the truck and jumped out. The path to the spring was short. Soon, he was there. He looked at the path beside the little pond area but saw no letter. In the pine high above, he saw the nest. The letter was not there either. He walked downstream a little and leaped, landing in a muddy area. One of his tennis shoes sank up to his ankle. Pulling the sneaker out of the muck, he walked up that side of the spring. The brush was thick, and he had to climb over some and under other branches.

Finally, Henry made it to the area across from the spring, and sure enough, there was the letter. As he reached down to grab it, a yellow jacket stung him in the hand. First, there was one, then there was three and then a whole gaggle of them. Not trying to swat them away, he grasped the letter and literally dove over a branch onto a clump of tall grass. Keeping his head low, he pushed through some brambles, and once on the other side, he noticed that the yellow jackets had abandoned him. His face was so swollen from the stings he could hardly see.

With one eye, he looked at the stamp with the golden daisy on it. Was that part of the story true also? Henry was now a believer of angels. Amelia's angel must have thought this letter important enough to show it to her while in her dream state. That could only mean one thing. With this letter and possibly a tiny bit more information, a little girl who needed her daddy more now than ever might just get her wish. Back at her room, the conversation continued.

Amelia was asking Rex another question, "My dear sweet bird, how did you come to get that letter? My angel said it was very important. It was so important that it can help to get my daddy out of prison. Won't that be wonderful, Rex? All of us can be home together again on the farm. And by the way, your secret is safe with me." She leaned close to the bird and whispered softly to him. Her words were so soft Cassandra could hardly make them out. "You have a beautiful family. You have a wife and four babies. Two of them are boys, and two are girls. You should be proud."

Cassandra looked around for Henry. He was nowhere to be found. If what the little girl told the bird was true, that letter had to be found fast. Even more urgent was the fact that if Rex understood even a small portion of the conversation with his mistress, he would go and find the letter if he saw it was missing.

"Where are you, Henry? If angels are as real as Amy says, then we need to find that letter before Rex does." Her words fell on empty ears. She reached for her phone and texted him.

"Henry, I know you were there and heard the story. I hope you are headed for the ranch right now to look for the letter because I am sure that as soon as this bird gets back to the ranch, he will go check on his family and probably notice something missing. Please respond."

Henry could not respond. He barely made it back to the house. His face was unrecognizable. Somehow, he managed to place the letter in the drawer where he originally intended to put it before closing it and diving into the nearby shower. He let the cold water pour over his head full force. He was soothed by it while, at the same time, shivering a bit as it soaked through his clothes all the way to his skin. It was too late when he remembered that his wallet was still in his pocket.

***

CHAPTER 6
Treatments for Cancer

Amelia drifted back into a state of unconsciousness. She was with her angel again. After Rex came and woke her up, the team working on her cancer called Cassandra into a conference room. They had the MRI scans and had placed them with other pertinent information into a presentation. She was shown the tumor in the brain of her little one. It looked bad. Before Amelia had drifted back to sleep as it were, they had checked out her vitals. She was now totally blind in her right eye. It was seriously affecting her motor skills. If that tumor persisted, she would not be able to function on any type of normal level. If the tumor was gone, they told the distraught mother there was no reason why she could not go home for visits and be part of the family from time to time.

Then the bad news came. It was the head surgeon who spoke, "The way it stands now, Cassandra, your daughter has at most six weeks to live. The complications from both types of cancer are complicating the treatment procedures. We would need to use two completely different methods of treatment for the two cancers. The problem with that is each separate treatment fights with the other, so in treating the brain tumor, the kidney cancer will grow worse. If we focus on the kidneys, then the brain tumor will increase in size. Already it is in danger of keeping her in a continual state of unconsciousness. It is a miracle that when the bird comes to see her, she responds as she does and seems to awaken and talk like a normal little girl."

Cassandra thought about what was being presented to her then spoke, "I have heard of miraculous natural treatments for cancer. I saw hundreds of testimonies that people have written. Many were as bad or worse than my little Amelia. Do you not have information on these natural methods or cures for cancer? If so, why won't you try them if you are so certain she is on her death bed? If she is going to die anyway, what harm could this cause?"

These were hard questions, ones the team had

heard many times, but the center had standards. Untested treatments could get them into trouble, so word came down from the administration to stick to the prescribed methods and procedures.

Dr. Riggins, the main physician on the case, had spent hours studying alternative methods. When he could get away, he would go out of the country to Mexico or other places and take in seminars. Secretly, he wanted to do something for this precious little girl. A tear trickled down his cheek. Cassandra noticed as he brushed it away then dismissed the rest of the team members before answering, "There may be something we can do, but if it is to be of any help to Amelia, we need to act fast. She would have to be discharged from here, and that is a problem. I will get back with you soon."

With that, he dismissed himself, heading for his office.

***

In her mind, Amelia was back with her guardian angel again. He was holding her in his arms. She looked up into his deep penetrating eyes. There was so much love radiating from them that she was lost within his gaze. She remembered what he had said, "I could heal you, Amelia. I could touch the tumor in your brain and make it go away, but then you would not be able to see me anymore. Your tumor is what enables you to talk to me."

For a long time, she lay there without speaking, soaking in the love that was flowing from him into her. Finally, she spoke, "The doctors say I am going to die, don't they?"

"Yes, that is the consensus from all the members on the team. The cancer that started in your kidneys has spread to other organs of your body. It is growing fast."

"If I am going to die, then could I make a request to you?" In her semi-dream state, she could see her angel with both eyes, even though in the physical world, she could only see out of one eye.

Her angel responded, "You certainly can make a request to me, but I am limited as to how much of that request I can grant. I follow the direction of a higher power, the Creator and Ruler of the universe. He is the one that makes the final decision."

"Is this the Jesus you were talking about, angel? I think I would like to see Him since you think so highly of Him. He must be very kind."

"Is that your request, Amelia?"

"No. My request is this. If I am going to die, can I experience one drop of forever?"

The angel had to ponder that for a while, trying to ascertain what she meant by one drop of forever. It could mean several things. One drop of forever experience could completely heal her of cancer and every other latent disease that might have been harboring itself in her genetic code. One drop of forever could be very potent. For all the times he had been a guardian angel to other humans over the thousands and thousands of years of his existence, he had never received a request like this.

After thinking about it for what seem like several minutes, he responded, "I will need to take your request to Jesus. He is the only one who can determine everything that would be involved in granting a request like that. You see, Jesus was at one time all knowing. He was also all present in all parts of time—past, present, and future. He was also all powerful. But when Jesus came down to this world and was born to Mary, He took on the physical properties of humans. To do that, He had to give up some of His former qualities. Am I talking in a language you cannot understand?" He looked lovingly into her eyes again to see if she understood what he was trying to say.

Amelia's eyes were closed. She had fallen into a deep sleep. Her nurse had given her some medication that put her to sleep. Perhaps it was a larger dose than should have been given to a girl as young as Amelia. The angel released his mental hold on her. She was sleeping soundly, so soundly, in fact, that her subconscious mind had slowed down also in its processing of the world around her.

The angel called out to another guardian angel that was looking after a boy in the next room who also had cancer, "Amelia has made a strange request, Kasterello. I need to make a trip back to heaven and consult with Jesus. My girl is sleeping soundly. Look in on her occasionally for me. I believe they gave her too high of a dose of sleep aid. If her heart rate falls much further, I believe you have the power to intervene. Jesus has some special things in mind for Amelia."

Kasterello responded. All the angels that had been left in heaven after a third of the entire company followed Lucifer knew each other on a first-name basis. Many had worked side by side over the centuries in missions Jesus had sent them on. Kasterello was no exception. Finally, he responded, "I will be glad to look in on her. They gave the same dosage to Benjamin, but he is about twenty pounds heavier than Amelia, and his body is not so deep into sleep as is hers. You told Amelia to call you Ademar instead of S. Ademarellian. Should I refer to you with the shorter or longer name now that you have voiced your preference?"

"You can call me Ademar. I kind of like a shorter name. Is there any message you want me to take to His Majesty?"

"Yes, let Him know I will come later with some news that He will like. I am sure if He wanted to, He could be listening in on our conversation if it is as you say that He has some special plans for Amelia. But it is hard to say for sure. Through the power of the Holy Spirit, He can do many, many things we probably do not understand. I will be so happy when He brings all this suffering to an end."

With that, Ademarellian was flying up toward the pearly gates of the Holy City, New Jerusalem. There was a short waiting line of angels when he approached the thrones of the Father and the Son. That would give this angel time to ponder a little bit longer on what the little girl meant by one drop of forever. Hope for this sweet little girl was beginning to form in his mind for the first time in several weeks. Perhaps angels have premonitions. Maybe they are given visions as were the great prophets of the Holy Bible.

In the mind of this angel, he saw Amelia home again. Though she was in a wheelchair, she was home and not in that room of death. Rex was there flying above her. She had her two arms outstretched, as if trying to reach up to him. In the background, the bright red barn was there with a fresh paint job. As it stood now, it was quite neglected. By Amelia's side was Barbara, the girl's favorite goat. It almost looked like it was pushing the wheelchair. Jesus would know if these pictures he was seeing would come to past. At least there was a little bit of hope forming in his intelligent mind.

When Cassandra got home with Rex, she saw Henry's truck in the yard. The bird was very glad to get back. As soon as she opened her door, he flew out heading up to his family.

She followed him with her eyes and spotted the tall pine tree with the nest. He was checking everything out. Inside, she found Henry lying on the couch. He was soaking wet. He had managed to find a plastic tablecloth from somewhere and place it down on the sofa first before plopping on it. She addressed him, and he grunted. His face was swollen. One eye would not open. He managed to turn his head and look at her, trying to say something. To her, it sounded like "Get help." He also had several welts on his arms where he had been stung. She called 911. Rex returned and came through the window. He immediately went to his stash and looked it over. He cocked his head first one way and then the other. Then he looked around the room. Soon he exited the window again.

Fifteen minutes later, the ambulance arrived. Henry had not been diagnosed with allergies to bee stings. There were just so many his body was having a hard time fighting off the poisons. They gave him a shot, and before long, he started to recover. Since his life did not appear to be in immediate danger, they decided to wait and see if a trip to emergency was necessary. After some twenty minutes, they departed. By then, Henry was able to speak clearly. Once the door closed behind them, he opened the conversation. "Sis, I would suggest you close the window so Rex cannot come in until you have finished reading the letter. It is in the drawer over there." He pointed to the antique desk then continued, "You might even stay away from the windows so the bird cannot see you with it."

"You sound like you know more about this letter than what you learned from the conversation Amelia had with Rex." She had the letter in her hand and traced her finger over the stamp. She also noticed the burns around the edges.

Henry responded, "When I was out doing the chores the other day, I saw that letter among Rex's treasures and got snoopy since I saw it was addressed to Joyce. I read it, and it is too bad this could not have been presented as evidence at the trial. Mike probably would never have gone to jail. Jim and Joyce were sleeping together. She even told him a story of her getting a divorce and marrying him. He fell for it hook, line, and sinker. He was going to confront Paul as mentioned in the letter at Vegas, and she could not have that happen because she was not getting a divorce. Last I heard, they were still together up in the log cabin there. Was that the one you featured first on your last log cabin calendar?"

"Yes, I believe it is come to think of it. That moon over the cabin was captured the night I gave birth to Amelia. It was such a beautiful night I set the camera to take several pictures a few minutes apart. Look, here are proofs." She went down three drawers from where he had placed the letter and pulled them out.

Henry slowly made his way over to a table where she spread them out along with the letter. He continued to explain how he came to know about the letter, "After reading it and placing it back in the envelope, Rex came in through the window and took it out of my hand. He said a few things then flew to his nest. I got some binoculars out and saw him tuck the letter between the nest and a branch. I did not know about the windstorm that blew it down by the stream. I lost sleep trying to figure out how to get it back. Then I heard the story Amelia told about her angel. I left and hurried up to the spot and found the letter, but that is where I ran into all the yellow jackets or whatever they were."

"We got it back, Henry. That is what is most important."

Henry noticed there were dates on the proofs along with the exact time the pictures were taken. He mentioned that to Cassandra, "According to the time these photos were taken, you should have seen tracks going up to the garage in the snow." He went through several of them and finally got to one where a car was coming into the driveway. It was long after the estimated time of the murder. These photos did not support Joyce's alibi about baking pies at home at the time of the murder. She was not home until well after the murder. Another photo showed she had exited and was halfway to the front door making tracks in the snow."

"This is proof she was not at home during the murder or anywhere close to it. If she had been, there would have been tracks in the snow. What can we do?"

"About the only option we have is to file papers to get Mike's sentence reduced based on new evidence. There is a lot of work I need to do in the morning at the office, but in the afternoon, I will go and get the proper papers to get this going." Henry selected four or five photos, while Cassandra finished reading the letter.

There was no opposition from Rex. With all those hungry mouths to feed, he and the Mrs. most likely had their beaks full trying to keep the little mouths stocked with insects.

After Henry appeared strong enough to walk around and alert enough to drive, he left. Cassandra decided she should go up and check on the goats. A walk in the open air would do her good. She did not get on the ATV by the door but walked up the hill. She was eating a banana. She was about to throw the peeling away when she remembered that goats eat almost anything. One or more of them would probably be glad for a bit of peeling. She first examined the nanny's when they came running up. There was a sore on one of the girl's nipples, so she got out the bag balm and gave it a generous portion. Next, she got out a brush and started to comb some burrs out of another one of the ladies' hide. Two little kids came running up, and she pulled out a couple of cubes and placed them in their open mouths. She also got down some oats and made certain every goat there got their share.

Normally Amelia would have helped with these chores, but there was a good chance after what the doctors stated that her daughter might never come home. She sat down on a bale of hay and started sobbing. She cried until there were no tears left. Several of the goats came and nestled up next to her. They were trying to comfort her in their own way. If only Mike was here to help her go through this dark valley, it would be so much easier to bear. She remembered the embrace he had given her while the police turned their backs. If Henry could figure out something to get him home again, it would be so wonderful! She would not have to go through this all by herself.

There was a radio Mike liked to listen to while working in the barn. It was within reach, so she turned it on. In the background, an old song was being sung: "All by myself, I don't want to be all by myself anymore." And she didn't.

She let her anger roar up to God. "You did this, God. Why? What did I ever do to have you treat me this way? You gave me the sweetest little girl a mother could ever wish for, and now You are going to take her away from me like you took my husband. When Grandma took me to church, they taught us the Lord's prayer. God, do You know what it says? How it starts out? I don't think You do! It starts out with the words: 'Our Father which art in heaven.' Some father you are. If you are such a God of love and allowed this to happen to me, you have got to be the worst Father ever! What father would treat any of his children the way you treated Mike and me? Do you like to see us cry like this?

"I just spent half an hour crying my heart out. I cried until no more tears came out. Did You comfort me? No. The goats did. They are more loving than You are. Is that the God of love I am supposed to worship of all the crazy things in the world? Why worship a God who claims to be a Father yet treats his children like garbage, like they are a rug under his feet? And what about my little girl? Answer that, one God almighty. What did she ever do to deserve even a minute of what You have allowed to happen to her? She is taking this far better than You deserve. I have not heard even one word of complaint out of my dear sweet, sweet Amelia."

Cassandra was crying again. And somehow there were still some tears left. She prostrated herself down on the barn floor, with her tears falling freely into the straw that was there. Another half hour or more passed. She was so exhausted that she cried herself to sleep. Barbara, Amelia's favorite goat, came and lay down beside her. She rested her head on the distraught mother's shoulder, and if goats can cry, Barbara was crying too.

When Casey got up, she drew some water for the kids and bid each mother goat goodnight. She gave each the same treatment. She would go up to them, kneel so she was close to their height, and wrap her arms around them, whispering some sweet nothings into their ears. In the house, she went straight to the bookshelf, took the Bible, and threw it across the room.

"There, God, You can have your old book. In the morning, I will take it out and let Barbara and her friends eat it for breakfast. That will teach You I am not someone to be trifled with." When she went over to gather it up, she saw six two dollar bills her grandmother had tucked there in the pages. They each had the years 1776–1976 on them. She gathered them up and cried out, "What have I done, God? I am blaming you for all of this when Grandma told me that when bad things come, it is not God that sends them but the devil. I am so sorry, God. Can You ever forgive me?"

The page in the Bible that was open had red letters written on it. That meant that Jesus Himself stated what was written there. She let her eyes rest on a passage. It seemed to rise out of the pages at her. It said, "Take heed that ye despise not one of these little ones; for I say unto you, that in heaven their angels do always behold the face of my Father which is in heaven. For the Son of man is come to save that which was lost" (Matthew 18:10–11).

Amelia had an angel. That was proven today when she described exactly where the letter was that might get Mike out of prison. Amelia's angel was real, and he always had access to the Father and the throne of grace. She placed the six bills back in the Bible. There was one for each year her little girl had lived on earth. After closing the cover, she reverently put it back in its place.

***

CHAPTER 7
Ameila's Trip to Heaven

Amelia was out for a long time. It did not seem like a long time to her though. One minute, she was in her angel's arms, and the next, she was back at the spring, crawling away from it up the hill where she knew Ademar was standing. He had his back toward her, so he could not see her struggling toward him on the rocky path. Was he talking to Jesus? He must be, otherwise, he would come down and pick her up in his arms again. To her, one drop of forever meant that she would experience going to the beautiful place angels come from—the place where Jesus had lived forever and would forever dwell. She strained her eyes to see, but Rex was there on a branch just in front of her. While she was waiting for the angel, why not get reacquainted with her pet. Without even thinking about it, she got up on her feet and walked toward him. Her legs were strong, and there was not any pain in her back. There was no dull hurt just below her tummy either. That sensation had evaporated away.

She was well again! Amelia tried running and was glad to see that her legs responded strongly. To try out her arms, she reached down and picked up a small rock. Turning back around, she heaved it toward the spring. She was rewarded with a big splash. This was wonderful! Had the angel gotten to Jesus, and had He granted her request? Had one drop of forever healed her? Rex started to chatter something to her as she came close to him. She noticed she was fully clothed with a towel draped over her shoulder. The bird took a little leap into the air, and with the help of his large wings, he easily made it to her shoulder. He gave his favorite ear lobe of hers a little nibble before speaking, "Ahmil happy! Ahmil run!"

And run she did. She ran down the path from the spring on two powerful legs. Rex had to raise his wings up and down to keep his balance. She ran all the way to the goat pen. Barbara came running to meet her with two little kids trying their best to keep up with their mom from behind. The girl embraced her much like her mother had. Amelia did not need to squat or kneel to do this. She was just the right size. She gave each of the babies some loving attention also. They were very tiny, so she was able to pick them up and hold them in her arms. Strong arms they were also. When she picked up the first little goat, Rex flew up in the air and kept circling around her. Soon his mate joined him. After putting the goats down, Rex rested on her shoulder again, and a pretty lady crow landed on a fence post not far away.

Rex spoke again in his rich, raven voice, "Lady, Ahmil. Pretty lady." And she was a pretty lady. She was a bit smaller than he was, but her feathers shone brightly in the sun. All the colors of the rainbow were reflected in them. After being introduced to the pretty lady, Amelia left the goat pen and looked up at the path. Her angel was walking toward her. She ran toward him, and he scooped her up in his mighty arms.

"I am well. See, Ademar? I can run like the wind again. My legs and arms are strong like they were before I got so sick. You must have talked to Jesus?"

The angel responded with a sad smile. Looking deep into her eyes with all the love he could muster, he spoke, "It is time for us to go, Amelia."

"Go where?" the little girl responded with some concern.

"We are going to the land of forever," he responded as he opened his large wings and was airborne.

Rex followed them up as high as he could fly before the oxygen got to thin. He was short of breath. Then he glided on some jet stream currents and watched until they were just a speck, then nothing. He returned to his pretty lady and hungry children.

After a fast flight where eventually stars came and went by them at lightning speed, they came to a beautiful tunnel of light. It was bright and very large. Astronomers claim that thirty thousand of our solar systems could rest side by side in the entrance of this tunnel of light. It was expansive. As they advanced along it, there was a bright spot up ahead that grew ever more brilliant and glorious the nearer they got.

Before them was a beautiful city. It was in the shape of a golden pyramid. It looked like a precious jewel as they came closer and closer. Soon, Amelia could see that at the base of the pyramid was a wall that surrounded the city. The wall was perfectly transparent with ripples of color added to increase its beauty. Amelia could see that on the side of the wall, they were approaching three giant gates. Each gate looked like a sparkling pearl. They were pure white again with rainbow colors mixed into them.

Ademar approached the middle gate. As they came nearer and nearer, it started moving to one side, disappearing into the wall. Brilliant, golden, glorious light first shown through the crack and then the whole once the gate was fully open. It was so bright the little girl's eyes took a long time to adjust to it. Then they were flying through it into a wondrous land of dazzling beauty. The angel set her down on a wide street of transparent gold. As soon as her feet hit the street, she started running again. She was running so swiftly her angel had to step up his pace by lengthening his strides. He was very tall. One would measure him at around seventeen feet according to earthly standards. He was smiling as he watched his precious treasure taking in the wonders of this glorious place.

Amelia came to a beautiful fountain in the middle of the street. Giant streams of pure, clear water shot hundreds of feet into the air and fell back down, causing a mist to rise out of the pond that was at their base. There were rainbows all around the fountain. Beautiful birds of paradise flew back and forth under the spray, allowing it to wet their feathers. Some would select a drop of water as it fell downward and dive for it, catching it in their beak just before it hit the water. In the pond were animals that loved to be wet. There were dolphins and seals along with hippopotamuses and rhinoceros. Occasionally, a whale would surface and add a spout of water shooting into the air like those of the fountain. A beautiful melody was heard throughout the entire city. It was sweet like the voices of angels singing. From time to time, the music would turn back on itself, and the echoes would rebound again and again off some sounding board it seemed before fading away.

There was that heavenly smile on the face of Amelia. When the angel saw it, he knew where it had come from. Jesus had given it to her in advance of her coming to heaven. He smiled and smiled as he watched her so strong, healthy, and happy in this land of wonder. He knew deep inside now that whatever happened with her disease process on earth, this place of wonder and beauty would be her eternal home throughout the ceaseless ages to come. And so, Ademar was satisfied. Earth with all its pain, suffering, and sorrow was only temporary. It would one day all pass away.

After playing in the water and taking special interest in a beautiful white dove that seemed to take to Amelia as Rex did, the little girl advanced more cautiously up the street, moving closer and closer to a great river up ahead. The dove landed on the same shoulder as Rex did and appeared to be right at home with the little girl. It was chattering away, chirping sweet nothings in her ear. Perhaps she understood the language of this bird. She understood the speech of Rex, so why not this dove? At the river, the girl paused and went down on her knees. She peered over the edge into the crystal water. Then she did something that caused the angel to become worried. She scooped up some of the water and took a long drink. That was usually forbidden by those who, in times past, had dreams and visions of this glorious place.

In their dreams, they were never allowed to drink the water of paradise. It was living water, imparting life to all who would drink it in the future. Ademar looked up high into the great arches of the city at the Father seated on His throne. He thought He saw him wink back, but maybe his eyes were playing tricks on him because he had never seen the Father wink at anyone during the ceaseless ages the angel had dwelt there.

After taking a drink, the little girl stood back on her feet and came slowly over to her angel. She looked way up at his face that towered above her and spoke a simple request, "Could you please take me to Jesus, Ademar? This place is so beautiful. I would like to go and see the One who made it, the One who did all of this." She stretched her little arms around in a big arch as if to encircle all the beauty as she spoke.

Reaching down, he scooped her up in his mighty arms, and in less time than it takes to write this, they were airborne, flying higher and higher in ever widening circles. The little girl was awestruck as she looked at the massive city stretching out in all directions below her. High above on earth, what would be a measurement by some as one thousand five hundred miles high was the mighty throne of God. It was not a single throne but a triple one. At the center, there sat a being that was so bright the little girl would never be able to see Him this side of heaven. He was the Father. On the right-hand side of the Father, Jesus sat. He was pouring over a book of light. That was the only way the little girl could describe it. It had pages, but they were not like the pages of a normal book one would read on earth but pages of light. On the pages, there were inscribed words, writing of some kind.

As she looked at the page Jesus was studying, understanding came into her mind. The words were names of people—people who either had lived back in the world where she came from or perhaps were living there now. Every now and then, Jesus would take a pen that bore ink that looked blood red. He would either blot out a name or blot out the strange words that appeared below the name. Again, understanding flooded into the mind of the little girl. It was blood He was using as ink. It was His blood, the very blood of Jesus. With His own blood, He either blotted out the name of a person or the writings below it, the record of the sins those people had committed while on earth.

The angel reached a platform with the little girl in his arms and rested. He bowed his head, not looking at Jesus and waited. Though Amelia could not see the Father, the angel could. The Bible states that none on earth are righteous, and if an unrighteous person looks at the form of the Father even once, they would cease to exist. Sinless angels who were not cast out of heaven when Lucifer fell could behold the form of the Father for they had never sinned. They were both righteous and holy, whereas humans are not. The angel, after bowing his head, looked up toward the father. He appeared to be communicating something to the angel.

During this entire time, Amelia was fascinated by the hand of Jesus holding the pen. There was a deep hole coming from His wrist. Why did Jesus have scars? Why was the skin of this beautiful person broken? On His noble brow, there were also marks that penetrated His skin. She could see that the scars on His brow went deep. Blood also showed from those holes in His head. From somewhere in her mind, a picture of Jesus hanging from a cross with a crown of thorns on His brow came to her remembrance, and then she knew. She knew that Jesus had once been on earth and had been nailed to a cross while there. At the thought of this beautiful person suffering on a cross, she started to cry. It was then that the lovely Jesus turned aside from His work and looked directly into her eyes.

His eyes showed such compassion they melted her heart. This Jesus was her Jesus. He had allowed Himself to die on the cross for her. Then He spoke with a voice so musical the vaults of heaven resounded and sprang forth with a new melody sweeter than anything anyone on earth has ever heard.

***

CHAPTER 8
The Anatomy of a
Murder ® Heaven

Back on the old dark earth, Nadra Betcher had managed to get a sample of Amelia's blood. Even now that she was running the test on it that came from the EU, an advanced computer system was scrolling out several possibilities as to which type of cancer was ravaging through this little girl's body. It compared the sample to those that had been collected and recorded since the test was developed. The computer was laboring, and the lab technician was running out of patience. She had stayed behind after the doors closed, claiming she had some unfinished business. There were security cameras recording everything she was doing. If someone got snoopy and decided to check up on her, she would need a good alibi. While the computer was doing its work, she was running different scenarios over her mind if someone, anyone was to question her later. Hopefully, they would not, then she would not need to voice the lie or lies that were being formulated.

Finally, the computer came to a conclusion. The tests confirmed Wilms tumor, but that was not all. There was a name of another type of cancer she was not well-versed in. It was called anaplastic astrocytoma. She ran a quick check on the browser of her cell phone on anaplastic astrocytoma. The survival rate in children who have this is around 28 percent. The sooner it is diagnosed, the better. For Amelia, this cancer would probably claim her life. She jotted the name down on a scrap of paper, took the samples, and disposed of them. She then tidied up the area where she had been working. She exited the room just as the night janitor started to make her rounds with all the cleaning equipment she used in her work. She gave a pleasant greeting and made her way to the big EXIT sign over the door.

The brain tumor in this little girl was very large. She was already unable to see out of one eye. There should be tremendous pressure in her skull, so much so that she should have chronic headaches. She would also have a hard time being able to think clearly. Nadra had heard of the large bird that went to visit her and of the conversations the little girl had with it. That story had traveled around in the medical circles for several days. Exceptions had been made for the crow to return. When there was no response from Amelia, they would bring the bird in—Rex was the name she called him by—and he would magically get her to awaken and start talking as if nothing were the matter.

Somehow the connection between Rex and Amelia was unusual, almost paranormal. There was also a rumor that she talked a lot about her angel. It was not surprising that with a tumor that size in her head, the little girl would be hallucinating. A friend of Cassandra, however, stated that the information the girl revealed while talking to the bird proved to be 100 percent accurate. Amelia's tumor was graded at III and was growing very rapidly. Removal by surgical means for this type of cancer is very difficult because of the tentacle-like fingers that grow into the nearby brain tissue. Nadra's heart sank as she made her way to the car. The only thing that would save Amelia's life now would be a miracle from heaven. If there was any hope at all, it was the fact this little girl seemed to have a connection to heaven through her angel, if there even were angels.

***

Henry recovered from the stings remarkably fast. Within a couple of days, he was going about his work as if nothing happened. He managed to research the type of paperwork that would need to be completed if there was to be reduced prison time for his brother. A retrial was probably out of the question since so much time had passed. He had hired a new secretary, and she filled all the details in, in short order. Going through the proper channels, he managed to present the evidence and paperwork and was assigned a case number. Since the organization was understaffed, they could not give him a date. In the meantime, they recommended that he hire a detective. A few names were suggested, and after another couple of days, Brad Thompson was hired. As a detective, he could access the information necessary to zero in on the activities of Joyce and those she had interacted with in the past as well as what was happening in her life at the present time.

Brad found that she had recently filed for a divorce. That in and of itself could add some turns and twists to the case. One thing was certain, this lady had been very busy. She had tried to cover up a lot of her activities, but as Brad dug deeper and deeper, a trail of evidence pointed back to her as the prime suspect in the murder. His brain was busy working out some details. Perhaps a civil trial might work. He remembered the case of OJ Simpson being acquitted of the murder of his ex-wife but losing in a civil trial that sent him to jail for years. He got on the phone to a lawyer friend of his to check it out. A reduced sentence would help Mike while letting Joyce go free. That was not enough though so far as justice was concerned. Since Joyce had committed the murder, she should pay for her crime. The civil trial might help with some recompense for Mike's suffering also. Being falsely accused and then going to prison unjustly should be worth something in the court of law.

The detective decided to do a stakeout not far from the log cabin of the former secretary. He got in his Jeep and drove out to her house. Once there, he noticed a For Sale sign out by the driveway. Three cars were up by the cabin. One of them belonged to a real estate agent. The realtor was showing the place at this very moment. He watched through his binoculars for several minutes. The clients appeared to be extremely interested in the property. Was there a way to stop the sale of property if the owners were under investigation for a crime? There should be. Brad needed to file a stop sale order quickly, or Joyce might move out of state, complicating the matter even more.

***

Joyce was not pleased when she was served with papers a few days later. Deep in her heart of hearts, she felt she had escaped the consequences of her crime. She was so close. Years had passed. People should have forgotten and moved on by now. But no, her secret sins appeared to be finding her out. She decided a trip away was what she needed. If she were gone for a few months more, perhaps she might escape from

63

this thing yet. It had taken its toll on her health. She appeared to have aged more than ten years during the last six. There was the constant nagging of a guilty conscience weighing her down and robbing her of sleep. Dark circles had formed under her eyes. She had all she could do to cover them with makeup.

For a time, Joyce had taken up another job. It was not that she needed to for her husband made good money. Also, she had managed to embezzle thousands and thousands of dollars out of Mike's business. Even now it was tucked away in a couple of offshore bank accounts just waiting for a day like this. As she was looking over the papers, her cell phone rang. It was the real estate lady. She was mad. The people that had looked at the cabin had put down the earnest money necessary to start the process going when a letter had come to her via registered mail with a stop-sale order.

"What is going on, Joyce? When we started this transaction, you had a clear title to the property. In your divorce settlement, your husband signed over full rights to you, and now I get this stop-sale order. Can you explain this?"

Another stab of pain shot through the guilty lady's heart as more complications came into her already troubled life. She had tried to justify her crime of killing Jim. It was his fault. Such a gullible guy as him should pay for his gullibility, should he not? If he weren't so stupid in matters of the heart, perhaps he should have been given a break, but he wasn't.

"I do not know, Barbara. What is going on? I thought everything was fine until I got—" She stopped midsentence, not wanting to let the realtor think there were multiple things going on in her life now. "Perhaps there has been a mistake. My ex-husband was not the sharpest tool on the rack, if you know what I mean. When it came to paperwork, he always had a hard time filling in even the simplest blanks. Like a person could explain it to him over and over, and he still would not get it. He probably missed something. He was so surprised when he was served the divorce papers. I wish I could have been looking from behind a tree and seen the expression on his face. He did not have a clue I knew he was cheating on me."

Barbara did not want to hear excuses. The commissions on the sale of this home would be substantial. To lose them was not in her plans. She shot an answer back, "Get in your Lexus and meet me at my office in twenty minutes with some answers, or I will file a lawsuit against you for withholding information from me in this sale. I am thinking if this does not go through, I should get the amount of my lost commissions as well as a few thousand dollars for the mental anguish you have caused me. If you are not there by the time specified, consider it as good as done from my standpoint."

Joyce was really distraught now. Too much was piling up on her too quickly. She had never been suicidal. The thought of taking her own life had not entered her mind. If one more thing happened though, it would push her over the top. The sales lady had not hung up, and neither had Joyce. The guilty lady exited the door and chanced to look up the sky. Several crows were flying around in circles. It was then she remembered the big one that came and took the letter from the flames. It was a letter that could convict her as the murderer. Someone had found that letter, and her dark past had finally caught up with her. She did not take long to decide. From her glovebox, she pulled out the 380 Sig Sauer, readied it, and before she could talk herself out of it, a shot rang out.

Barbara heard the sound of a gun going off. "Are you still there, Joyce? I heard a shot. What was that all about?" A deathly silence was the only response that came back to her. "Joyce, speak to me, please! Has something bad happened to you? Did your ex show up? Do I need to call 911? Where are you? Are you at home?" Not knowing what else to do, she dialed 911 and gave the address of Joyce's home to the person that was on the other end of the line.

***

Brad was kind of snoopy. He had hired someone to serve the papers to Joyce because the law recommended strongly that he not do it. Something about a conflict of interest. He watched the carrier from the same place he had been when he stalked the cabin out earlier in the week. Joyce had taken the envelope. A strange look had crossed her face. Not knowing what else to do after the guy left, she had gone inside the cabin.

Several minutes passed, Brad was about ready to leave when the door opened again, and she emerged with her cellphone. She appeared to be talking with someone. The discussion was heated. The expression on her face appeared to confirm that, so he hung around a little bit longer. What happened next was the most surprising event he had ever witnessed in his life. Joyce opened the glovebox in her vehicle, readied a small pistol, and shot herself. To his dying day, that picture could never be erased from his mind. 911 got two calls within seconds of each other. Both listed the same address. One was to report a shot that was heard from there, and the other was to report a death by suicide. Crime never pays.

A person can hope to escape paying the consequences of their sins, but in the end, justice will be served. In the books of heaven, there is a faithful record being kept of every action a person takes. Every secret is written down in heaven's language. That was what Jesus was reviewing when a certain little girl, through the means of a dream, entered His presence.

There is a passage in the Bible that the Master spoke to His disciples while still on earth. You can read it in John 14:1–3. It reads something like this: "Let not your heart be troubled: ye believe in God, believe also in me. In my Father's house are many mansions: if it were not so, I would have told you. I go and prepare a place for you. And if I go and prepare a place for you, I will come again, and receive you unto myself; that where I am, there ye may be also." Jesus now paraphrased this as He looked deep into the 'troubled' eyes of Amelia.

Back on earth, His compassion would go out to people like this. It was said there were entire villages that had no one sick once He passed through them. He healed everyone. His musical voice now calmed the little girl, and she stopped crying. The purest love she had ever seen was in His eyes as He spoke, "Do not cry, Amelia. Don't be troubled. You are in My Father's house. There are many mansions here. There is one that I prepared just for you. Soon I am going back to your world to gather all the people who believed first in My Father than in Me. You believe in Me because you have seen me. When I gather all My people together to bring them here, you will be with them. I love you so much. I can hardly wait until the day you and your mom and dad will all be together with Me here in this beautiful city. Would you like to go and see the mansion I made especially for you?"

The little girl had been watching Him closely, taking in every word. She did not miss a single one. As He spoke, a wonderful peace came over her. She knew this friend was her forever friend, and that He would never leave her or forsake her. Even if the disease that was taking over her little body claimed her life, she would be able to face it bravely because she knew that in time, Jesus would be there to take her in His mighty arms, just as He did now. He opened them wide, and she was there cradled close to His heart. He was smiling down at her, and that sweet forever smile that was hers and hers alone spread over her face. Gone now were the tears.

"I would love to go see my mansion. Will you take me, or will my special angel Ademar? You are so very busy I would not want to take up any of your precious time if You can't spare any. I would be fine with Ademar. We are very good friends."

"I will be taking you, Amelia," Jesus responded as He rose from His throne and started toward a large platform beneath it.

To the little girl, it looked like a great sea of glass. In Revelation 7 and 14, there are some special people from earth who will one day stand on it and sing a song to Jesus and all heaven—a song that even the angels cannot sing, for angels can never experience the joy that the salvation of one person brings.

In a short time, the two were at the entrance of several beautiful homes. They paused a moment to look up at the glory of the sight before them. A golden street wound up to an archway made of transparent jasper. The colors of the archway were deep reds and oranges with dashes of yellow. At the top of the arch were inscribed the words HOLINESS TO THE LORD. Above the archway, stretching miles into the sky, were the beautiful homes of the saints on this side of the city.

The view took Amelia's breath away. Her eyes, so darkened on earth, seemed starved for each beautiful scene. She had to touch, feel, and smell everything to see if it was real. She stood staring at the beauty before her for a long, long time, then spoke. "These are the most beautiful homes in all of heaven!" she exclaimed in a whispered, reverent tone.

"They are beautiful," responded Jesus, "and higher than any mountain on earth. They are more glorious than ten of your suns."

Among the gardens, brilliant birds swung from trailing vines loaded with grapes and fruits of rarest beauty. Their unceasing songs ascended to God with joy unquenchable. Other plants of varying shades of green and gold were interspersed among the flowers.

Finally, the little girl cried out from the depths of her very soul. "Thank You, Jesus. Thank You and I Love You and I thank You again. Thank You for allowing me to see this place."

As if in a dreamland, Amelia and Jesus started up the golden street into the mansions above. Higher and higher they went. The view changed from every angle. Wide verandas curved into spiraling stairs and winding hallways. Gold and silver archways framed the entrances to intersecting terraces and spacious courtyards. Glistening stairways opened into living gardens with flowing waterfalls and vibrant green lawns. When they spoke out loud, their voice returned to them, bouncing off the polished pillars and crystal walls.

A hundred kinds of fruits spread their beauty before any who wished to eat them. Plums, peaches, apricots, and apples of gold and silver beaconed to the hungry traveler. "Partake and be filled." The buzzing of bees blended with the beating wings of the ruby-throated hummingbird. A little sparrow sang from his perch on the flowering branches of the wisteria vine. Gems of rarity and beauty sparkled from every nook and cranny. Amelia found herself raising her voice with the singing birds as they went ever higher. Soon, they were at the door of an especially beautiful home.

"This is the home I made just for you, Amelia. It has many of your favorite things in it." He touched the door and stepped back out of the way as it disappeared into the wall.

The first thing that met her was Rex. At least it looked like Rex. This bird seemed to know all about the girl in front of him. He even spoke, and my oh my, if it truly was Rex, his vocabulary had increased a lot. Where on earth Rex could speak a few words that made sense part of the time, this Rex could carry on detailed conversations with anyone who would take time to listen to him. And the little girl did listen with the broadest, most glorious smile any little six-year-old has ever smiled. It was a smile that came all the way up to her face again from all the way down in her heart.

"Ms. Amelia." Somehow, he had learned to pronounce her name perfectly in every detail. "What has led to this unexpected presence of my beautiful friend? I was not expecting you so soon."

"No, Rex. It is not what has led me to your presence. It is who brought me here, Jesus."

"You mean, the Master is here at this very moment?"

The large black bird bowed his head slightly as he voiced the word, "Master." All of heavens reverenced that name above all names—the one that on earth meant, "You will call His name Jesus for He will save His people from their sins." The bird hopped into the air and flew backwards slightly to a golden perch suspended from the ceiling with two silver chains. The perch had tiny gems of beautiful colors embedded in them.

Jesus appeared at the door and spoke to the bird, "Would you like the pleasure of showing Amelia her beautiful home?" He looked deep into the dark beady eyes of the raven as He spoke.

"It would be my pleasure, Master, but I am sure you could do a better job since you designed and built it all."

Jesus nodded to the bird to carry on, and he hopped gently down, resting on the little girl. Not one of his feet dug into her shoulder. She did not even need a towel. Her ear lobe was just too tempting, and he had to give it a little nibble.

There were windows in the home framed in a ruby red trim. They looked out over the vast city stretching out for miles and miles all around them. This was where he first led the girl. Somehow, she seemed to know the direction he wanted her to go without him having to ask her. Outside the window was a zip line. The bird showed her a little panel she could put coordinates in that would take her at near lightning speed to several places in the city. Somehow understanding came to her mind, but she was not ready for that adventure yet. Perhaps when the time came to leave, she would sadly need to use it to take it to where Ademar waited for the return trip home.

On a table at the center were several types of fruits someone had gathered from the many trees around the mansion. There was a couch that appeared to be made of pearls. The iridescence showed a heavenly light. Amelia was not tired, but she wanted to see what it felt like. She made her way over to it, reaching out a finger she touched it. It did not feel solid at all. So, without giving it the slightest thought, she took a little hop into the air and plunked herself down. It perfectly conformed to the curvature of her body the moment she landed. From that position, she looked up into the face of Jesus. He was smiling, taking pleasure in her delight as each new discovery came to her attention.

She had a robe room, a closet, a place to prepare food,

and several chairs that would go into a wall or fold out with a simple touch of the finger. Her home could probably hold at least twenty people, if need be, or perhaps more. There were sparkling gems hanging from the corners of the room. As the rays of light from outside entered the home, they would glitter, sending out rainbows all over the spacious rooms. Today with Jesus there, however, they put on a special display of glory. Each one was giving their praise to their maker.

"What are all these strange-looking gadgets, Rex? I have never seen anything like them. They are out of this world."

"They are from out of this world or out of heaven, Amelia. When you come here in the future and travel to many other worlds Jesus has made, you will make many friends. Your new friends will each want to give you a gift. These are some of the gifts you will receive once this place becomes your permanent dwelling." The bird was very pleased with himself for having strung so many words that made so much sense together.

There were several musical instruments in her house. Of course, there was a harp. Everyone who goes to heaven will have a harp of their very own and know how to play it. There were some woodwinds and brass instruments that were just waiting for someone with the time to play to pick them up and enjoy. One special instrument caught the little girl's attention. Her grandmother had a piano. Back in the days when she visited, the little girl would sit down and make music. She was given a good ear for music too.

A couple of years before her cancer came, she had picked out her first song on that piano much to the amazement of those in the room. She had the uncanny ability to play by ear as it is called on earth—that is, to play without needing to read notes on a music score. Rex directed her over to the crystal piano. One could look right through it and see all the internal workings. They were intricate and perfectly orchestrated.

Jesus pulled the bench out for her, and as she seated herself, he pushed it in to the exact place where it was most comfortable for her. She thought a few minutes before letting her little fingers touch the keys. Then the melody came. It was like no song one has played on earth, but the way she performed was perfect. Each note was hit with precision and definition. The song swelled louder and louder, going out the open windows and bouncing back to the occupants of the room in echoes that added depth to the whole. It was like an entire orchestra was playing along with the little girl there in the beautiful home she would one day occupy. After the music died away, she went to her little sofa and fell asleep. She was awakened with Rex—the Rex from her own world nibbling on her ear lobe.

The doctors could not understand how a tumor of such a massive size, one that was crushing out the life of this precious child of the kingdom, could disappear overnight. Though she still had the Wilms tumors, the brain tumor was completely gone. With it no longer a problem, it was quite possible she would finally be able to go home. Would she remember her dream trip to heaven and the beautiful mansion Jesus had taken her to? Heaven only knows. Was one drop of forever enough to bring about a full cure of all her cancer symptoms? You do know that forever cannot die, so what would some of forever do in your body? What does one drop of forever even mean?

EPILOGUE

Amelia was finally home. After going through several hours of physical therapy and chemotherapy treatments, she was able to do things for herself. She could walk a little but went around in her wheelchair most of the time. Barbara became so tame she would follow the girl around the yard, even pushing the chair if her mistress asked her to. Then she would walk herself back to the barn when the girl went inside. There was a one-way door her daddy had made for this special pet.

Yes, Amelia's daddy was finally home also. The paperwork had gone through, and although he was on probation, he was free to do anything normal dads do for their kids when they are not working. I say kids because beside the goat kids, Cassandra was expecting a baby boy, and Amelia would have a little brother soon. Mike was also allowed to go back to work much to Henry's relief. Together, the brothers expanded the business and started some franchises in different parts of the country.

Rex was his own usual self, getting into mischief as much as ever, plus some of his kids became quite the pests also. They loved playing tricks on the girl in the wheelchair. She had to watch everything, or it would be packed off to who knows where. Another coat of red paint was put on the barn, and it became the cover photo of a brand-new calendar.

Cassandra was making quite a name for herself. She even published a biography describing her story of being a single mother with a daughter diagnosed with terminal cancer. Ademar never came back. Oh, he was around for sure. He was not going to let anything happen to his precious Amelia. He would fight off a thousand wicked angels if necessary. Have them try to harm even one hair on her head—hairs that were at best few and far between--and they would know what bullets of glory felt like penetrating their deteriorating forms.

Amelia did eventually grow her hair back. When it went away, it was straight; but when it grew back, it came in all curly. That was not a problem for her. She kept smiling her way through the world. By the way, if you ever happen to be in the Bozeman area of Montana and you see a smile that can melt the clouds away on a rainy day, a smile that comes up to the face of a beautiful girl from all the way down in her heart, perhaps it will be Amelia. One never knows who you might encounter. Maybe it will even be an angel.